GUIDELINES FOR LIFE

Personal and Social Issues in World Religions

Mel Thompson

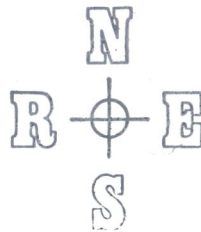

N
R◆E
S

Hodder & Stoughton
LONDON SYDNEY AUCKLAND TORONTO

British Library Cataloguing in Publication Data
Thompson, M. R. (Melvyn Rodney), *1946–*
   Guidelines : personal and social issues in world
   religions.
   1. Society. Role of religion
   I. Title
   306.6

   ISBN 0 340 51950 9

First published 1990

© 1990 Mel Thompson

Typeset by Wearside Tradespools, Fulwell, Sunderland
Printed in Great Britain for the educational publishing division of
Hodder and Stoughton Ltd, Mill Road, Dunton Green, Sevenoaks, Kent
by St Edmunsbury Press, Bury St Edmunds.

Contents

Foreword

TO THE TEACHER

Many books give details of personal and social issues, and some attach to them Christian comments and biblical references. These may be valuable as a basis for study, but they do not give an adequate account of the moral guidelines offered by the major world religions. *Guidelines for Life* aims to go further, and to provide an understanding of the religious principles and values which influence the choices people make when confronted by personal or social issues. It is designed to meet the needs of many GCSE syllabi, and to provide a multifaith religious component for Personal and Social Education.

As you will see from the 'To the student' note, this book does not attempt to convey detailed knowledge of each of the issues, but gives only sufficient information to allow students to appreciate how each set of guidelines may be applied to practical situations.

Questions in the text seek to stimulate an evaluation of the material, but, in answering them, students are likely to show whether or not they have an adequate understanding of the moral guidelines and the religious principles that lie behind them.

Questions are set within shaded boxes, and are of two kinds:

- Some encourage evaluation of a particular guideline in response to the 'Evaluation' criterion at GCSE.

- Others are more general and may provide a starting point for discussion, especially if the book is being used as a religious component within Personal and Social Education.

TO THE STUDENT

This book sets out the rules and values by which the six major world religions help people to decide how they should live, and what choices they should make about their personal and social life.

Whether you are using this book as part of a course on Personal and Social Education or for Religious Studies at GCSE, you should have up-to-date facts about family life, peace and conflict or the way in which humankind is treating the environment. These facts are constantly changing, and you will need to research them yourself, from textbooks, from a library or from the newspapers.

This book gives you the guidelines by which you can interpret those facts and relate them to the teachings of the world's religions.

An outline of the personal and social issues covered in this way is given on pages 7–10.

Guidelines for Life has been written to make it easy for you to research particular issues thematically, across the religions, because each of the chapters is divided up in the same way. For example, you could take the issue of warfare and easily move from a section on Jewish attitudes to sections on Buddhist or Hindu attitudes. In the opening section on each religion, there is an outline of its general guidelines, which are then applied to each issue. This will help you to understand the foundation for the ideas and attitudes of the different religions presented in this book.

Introduction

ASKING WHY

> You shouldn't do that!

> Why not?

> Because it's wrong!

> Why is it wrong?

> Because I say so!

If you have younger brothers or sisters, you may try to stop them doing something you believe to be wrong and become infuriated when they keep on asking 'Why?'. Your sense of authority is challenged; you are forced to think about your reasons for deciding that something is either right or wrong; you have to sort out questions about what is important, what has value, what you believe in. Perhaps you just feel that something is wrong without knowing why. Perhaps you were taught that it was wrong when you were younger. Perhaps you just want to assert your authority. Perhaps your motives are mixed. You may be tempted to answer 'Because I say so!' rather than argue it through. You may even find parents or teachers who give a similar answer if you challenge them!

In this book we shall be looking at guidelines – the beliefs and values by which people decide what is good or bad, right or wrong. We all have guidelines, but we may not stop to think about them. **You can find your personal guidelines by asking yourself 'Why?' everytime you think something is right or wrong.**

LOOKING FOR RESULTS?

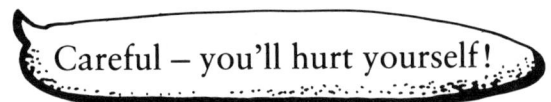

> Careful – you'll hurt yourself!

Sometimes you decide for or against an action according to its expected results. If you do not want to suffer the consequences of an action, you do not do it, however tempting it may seem in itself.

Arguments of this sort depend on the accuracy with which you can predict results. The more certain you are about the result of an action, the stronger may be your case for saying that it is either right or wrong.

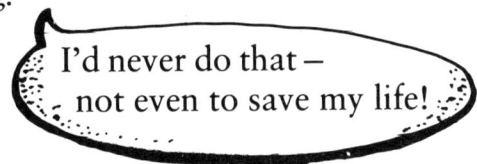

> I'd never do that –
> not even to save my life!

On other occasions, the result of an action may be less important than the idea that it is absolutely right or wrong in itself. For example, telling a lie or cheating in a test might, in the short term, produce some rather pleasant consequences (e.g. you may be congratulated for something you have not done), but you might still want to say that it is wrong to lie or cheat.

Arguments of this sort tend to start with **absolute rules** (e.g. it is always wrong to kill), but may offer **exceptions** (e.g. you may kill in self-defence, or to save the life of an innocent person).

Sometimes, one sort of argument will lead into the other. You may start with an absolute rule that you should tell the truth; but when asked why, you may point out that, if everyone told lies, there would be chaos – which is an argument based on results. Similarly, telling a small child not to pick up a kitten by its tail may sound as if it is based on the result (that the animal will be hurt), but it also depends on the general rule that it is wrong to inflict pain.

Whenever you have to decide between right and wrong, you are making a **moral choice**; and when you try to explain or comment on a moral choice, you are doing **'ethics'**. Ethical arguments are based on the values and attitudes you hold, the guidelines which influence how you choose to live.

- Working with a partner, each of you should think of something which you believe to be morally wrong, and then write 'I think it is wrong to _____' at the top of a sheet of paper. Your partner should then keep asking 'Why?' or 'So what?' to every explanation you give, while you note down the stages of your reasoning. Do this until you arrive at the general principles and values on which your moral statement was based.

EXAMPLE:

I think it is wrong to eat meat.

Why?

Because I don't want to kill animals.

Why?

Because it involves pain, and destroys life.

So what?

Because I think life is valuable.

Why?

I think my life is valuable, so that should apply to all other people and animals.

So?

I wouldn't want to be killed and eaten, so its not fair to do it to another animal.

So what are your principles and values?

Do not do to any other creature what you do not want done to yourself. All life is of value and should not be harmed.

Now reverse your roles and question what your partner believes to be wrong.

FACTS AND VALUES

In order to make a choice, you need two things: facts and values. There are many facts available on world-wide ethical issues – from abortion and euthanasia to world poverty and care of the environment. Unless you know the facts about a particular issue, you will not be able to decide what you should do about it. Equally, if you do not understand the values and principles upon which you and other people base your choices, you will not be able to see why different people come to different conclusions, even when presented with exactly the same facts.

Everyone else does it!

That doesn't mean it's right!

Facts are not enough to explain or excuse what you do. Suppose you were in court, accused of mugging a pedestrian. Armed only with facts to explain your behaviour, you might say, 'Violent crime against individuals is increasing in this country'. But if you think that this fact will explain and excuse your action, you should not be surprised if the judge says 'So is the prison population', as a reason for sending you to gaol. **Statistics in themselves do not show if an action is right or wrong.**

FOUR KINDS OF ACTION

1 Moral
An action is morally right, if it is done for a reason, and follows from the values and beliefs of the person who does it.

2 Immoral
An action is immoral if it goes against the known principles of right or wrong by which a person lives.

I think it's wrong. Therefore, for me, it would be immoral.

I live by different values. For me it would be morally right.

Of course, one person may think that a thing is morally right, while another may think that the same thing is immoral and therefore wrong. Society as a whole may approve of something (e.g. eating meat) while an individual (a vegetarian) thinks that it is wrong. Or society may disapprove of something (e.g. robbing a rich person in order to support a charity), while an individual (e.g. Robin Hood) may think it right.

3 Amoral

Now look what he's done!

Don't blame him; he's too young to understand.

If a person has no understanding of right or wrong, he or she cannot be blamed for his or her actions. A small child taking someone else's sweet, does not yet understand that it is wrong to steal. Such actions are called 'amoral' (i.e. resulting from having no morality).

4 Non-moral

It's not my fault!

I couldn't help it!

The vast majority of actions (even very important ones) are not concerned with right or wrong. It is not morally wrong to have a car accident (although the consequences may be terrible); it only becomes a moral issue if the accident is caused through careless driving, drunkenness, or deliberately risking life by using a vehicle which is unroadworthy. You cannot be blamed for something which was outside your control and about which you had no choice.

- Here are three actions. State whether you think each is moral, immoral, amoral or non-moral, and give your reasons.

  - Trespassing on private property in order to rescue a friend who has a broken leg.
  - Giving totally wrong directions to a lost motorist, because you suddenly got your 'left' and 'right' muddled.
  - Buying a large amount of a food because you know that it will soon be in short supply.

- Compare your answers with someone else's. If they are different, discuss together and note down the different reasoning or values that you have used in coming to your decision.

ARE WE FREE TO CHOOSE?

All moral language about actions being 'right', or about what people 'ought' to do, assumes that we are free to choose whether to do them or not. The religions described in this book all claim that people are free to follow or to reject their guidelines, but some people argue that everything we do is determined.

When scientists examine the parts of an atom, or the behaviour of an animal, they assume that everything they find has a cause. Therefore, if we knew every detail of what had happened in the past, we could predict exactly what would take place in the future.

If we apply this to personal and social issues, it seems that everything is determined by the past, and we are not free to choose what we do.

When other people look at us, they may give explanations for everything we do. To them, we may seem to be absolutely controlled by all the physical laws that work on us, but (at the same time) we experience ourselves as free to act and to make moral choices.

Typical! I just knew you'd do that!

- Has anyone ever said that to you? Either remember (or imagine) a situation where you have chosen to do something (or perhaps to buy something to wear) and a friend or relative has said that they could have predicted your choice.

  - Did you think you were free to make your choice?
  - What influences were you conscious of?
  - Was there anything that you were unaware of at the time, but which, on reflection, might have influenced your choice?

REWARDS AND PUNISHMENTS

People who do what is wrong in the eyes of the society in which they live may be punished. Here are five reasons that may be given for it:

1 Society may need to be **protected** from a person who is dangerous or violent. Punishment may prevent him or her from doing any more harm.

2 If one person is seen to be punished, it may **deter others** from committing the same crime.
3 It may **reform** the person who has done wrong, so that he or she will not want or need to commit the crime again.
4 It may be seen as a just **retribution** for the wrong that has been done. In other words, a person simply deserves to be punished.
5 It may be necessary to punish wrong-doers in order to **vindicate the law** (i.e. to show that the law is right and deserves respect). In other words, if everyone got away with doing just what they liked, there would be no respect for any law or authority.

> - For each of the above reasons for punishment, choose a crime and select an appropriate punishment.

Religions also offer rewards or punishments to those who obey or disobey the rules and values on which they are based. This may happen in three ways:

1 A religion may teach that, after death, a person may experience Heaven or Hell (the one offering a reward, the other punishment for what has been done during this life). Similarly, religions that teach rebirth, claim that the next life will depend upon good or bad actions performed in this one.
2 Religions may also teach that a follower may gain happiness, peace of mind, or personal success in this life as a result of following their guidelines.
3 Where religious laws are also the laws of that country (e.g. Muslim countries like Saudi Arabia, Iran or Pakistan), a person may be punished in the courts for disobeying what others would see as a religious rule (Muslims believe that their religion involves the whole of life, not just 'religious' activities).

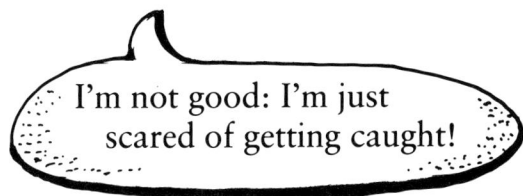

I'm not good: I'm just scared of getting caught!

Most religious people would argue that you should do the right thing for its own sake, not just because of a threat or reward.

WHO SHOULD DO IT?

The same action may be seen as right if done by one person, and wrong if done by another. For example, there is nothing wrong in an adult getting married or driving a car, but neither is allowed if you are under age. A surgeon may take a sharp knife and cut open a complete stranger, and that will be considered a good thing to do. Even if the patient dies, the surgeon will not be blamed, unless it can be shown that he or she acted negligently. On the other hand, if an un-trained person cut someone open, he or she might be accused of wounding or murder. But what if there was an emergency, with no time to get a surgeon, and you were the only person who could help? Would it be right for you to attempt an operation?

Operate!

Who? Me?

It is the situation, the intention of the person who does it, and the appropriateness of the action which may help us to decide if it is right or wrong. **Each action needs to be set in its context.**

> - Think of an action for which you could be punished, but which would be acceptable if done by someone else. Explain carefully the differences involved.
> - Can you think of an action which you would be permitted to do in one situation, but for which you could be punished if you did it in some other context?

In the same way, an action may be considered right for a follower of one religion, but it would be considered wrong if done by a follower of another.

WORLD RELIGIONS AND MORAL CHOICE

All people make choices: all, whether they think about them or not, have some sort of moral values by which they live. For a member of one of the world religions, these values will be influenced by the beliefs and practices of that religion.

> It's nothing to do with religion; it's just that people in this country don't think it's fair!

> But where did your idea of fairness come from?

> You shouldn't do that, it's against your religion!

> I'm not *that* religious. I'm like everyone else, really.

A non-religious person may claim that his or her moral principles come as a result of careful thought and do not depend upon religion. But very often, the values that are found in a society have developed gradually, as a result of religion (e.g. many values and attitudes expressed by non-religious people in Western countries, reflect the long history of Christian influence, even where they reject the Christian religion itself). **In this way, religious ideas influence people who, in other respects, have nothing to do with religion.**

Almost four-fifths of the world's population claim to have some sort of religious belief, and the guidelines for life offered by the six major world religions described in this book exert an influence throughout the world.

In looking at the lifestyle of religious believers, you may want to say 'all Christians believe that people are created equal in the sight of God and should be treated as such' or 'Buddhists never use violence'. But then you may find a South African Christian who supports apartheid, or a Buddhist monk who joins in a violent demonstration against the Chinese control of Tibet. Therefore, it is often better to say 'Some Christians believe . . .' or 'Most Buddhists think that . . .'. But why do religious people differ in this way? Here are two reasons:

1 Within a religion, some values may conflict with others, and a believer has to make a choice, or strike a balance between them (e.g. Christians would accept the idea that a person should honour mother and father, but also that Jesus told his followers to be prepared to leave their families in order to follow him).

2 The values given in a person's religion may go against those of the society in which he or she lives. Choices have to be made, and these depend on how strongly the person feels about his or her religion, and the amount of social pressure to be like everyone else (e.g. young Hindus, Muslims or Sikhs, living in Britain, may find that their families and religious traditions suggest that they need help in finding a suitable marriage partner; but friends at school, and people they see on television, say that they should marry only after they fall in love).

There may always be exceptions to a rule. **The important thing is to know the religious principles by which each person comes to his or her own conclusion.**

No two people are exactly alike, but members of a religious group hold certain values in common, and it is these guidelines for life that we shall be exploring.

- Can you think of a religious value or rule that may influence non-religious people in society?

- Are there any values commonly held in society as a whole which might cause problems for a religious person? (e.g. about making money, or the choice of a career).

The issues

In this book we shall examine the way in which religious guidelines are applied to a variety of personal and social issues. These issues may be divided into three groups:

MARRIAGE AND THE FAMILY

Some of the issues here are:
- remaining single
- the choice of a marriage partner
- promises made at a wedding
- contraception
- bringing up children
- sex outside marriage
- divorce
- care of the elderly
- abortion and euthanasia

You may want to consider the things that can threaten a marriage: financial problems; lack of time together; the pressures of work; and the failure of marriage to live up to a person's hopes for it. The Divorce Law Reform Act, which came into force in Britain in 1971, described the basis for divorce as the 'irretrievable breakdown' of marriage. How do you decide when this has happened? All religions offer guidelines on marriage.

Both children and old people have special needs. How they are treated may depend on the sort of family in which they live. In some countries most people live in nuclear families – mother, father and children, living apart from other relatives. In other places, people live in extended families, with married children and grandchildren living together in their parents' home. There are also single-parent families, and people living alone. Religious attitudes towards individuals and family life influence the way in which people live together in society.

A very special day: all religions offer guidelines about marriage and family life. But what promises should you make to your partner, and what should you do if a marriage goes wrong?

At eighteen weeks, this unborn baby sucks its thumb in the womb. Is it ever right to kill a child like this by having an abortion? All the world religions have things to say about the value of human life.

Some choices involve life or death. Should new life be prevented by using contraceptives? Is it ever right to end the life of an unborn child through abortion and if so, in what circumstances? Should a person be helped to die if, for any reason, he or she feels that life is unbearable? What have religions got to say about the value of human life?

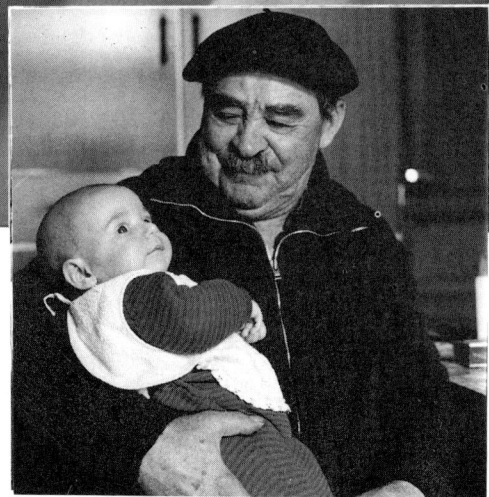

Old people and children have a great deal to give one another. How is family life best organised to take into account their special contribution and their needs?

PEACE AND CONFLICT

Some of the issues here are:
- individual violence
- capital punishment
- human rights
- political action
- non-violent protest
- accepting the authority of the state
- warfare

Is it ever right to use violence against another person, or for one country to go to war against another? We will see that the world religions offer very different views on this issue.

In the First World War, about ten million people were killed. The majority of them were in the armed forces – either professional soldiers, volunteers or conscripts (people required to do military service). In the Second World War, as well as seventeen million military personnel, thirty-four million ordinary civilians were killed. Modern warfare therefore involves everyone and the destruction it brings is greater than anything known in the past.

Guidelines that limit the amount of force that should be used against an enemy, can be applied to all kinds of weapons. This book will not consider nuclear weapons as a separate issue, although it may be important for you to apply the guidelines to the threat of their use.

Modern warfare affects everyone; not just those who are trained to fight. Rescue workers hunt in the rubble of a school, bombed during the Second World War. They recovered the bodies of twenty children. (Catford, London; 1943)

HUMANKIND AND NATURE

Some of the issues here are:
- care of the environment
- work and leisure
- health, food and drink
- the abuse of alcohol and drugs
- the use of natural resources
- world development
- animal rights

People are becoming increasingly aware of the danger of polluting the environment or of using its resources to the point of exhaustion. This can bring about human disaster, as is illustrated in this extract from *Christian Aid News*.

Christian Aid News
Nature's warning

RECENT events in Bangladesh and Sudan point to the dangers we all face when the fragile systems of nature on which we depend are attacked.

The floods were not natural disasters brought about by freak weather or acts of God. They were man-made tragedies whose causes are ignored.

In Africa, poverty is forcing villagers to strip their surroundings of trees and greenery to provide fuel and fodder. Rain water is not absorbed and soil is more easily washed away in seasonal storms. River levels rise and floods occur.

In India and Nepal, the richly forested slopes of the Himalayas have been greedily logged by commercial companies for years without any care for replanting. When the monsoon strikes, the bare soil tumbles into the valleys, clogs river beds and causes sudden floods. A series of bigger and bigger floods has descended on Bangladesh in recent years and devastated its fragile economy.

We can do more than mourn as we once again help those affected to rebuild their lives. We can insist that our government and industries take care of the environment and put resources into protecting it. We can also speak up for those who have no voice.

Acid rain and the exploitation of land and forests are well understood hazards to life. But we must all work to remove them before it is too late.

What about human life? How should we treat our own bodies? How should we respond to the inequalities of wealth and poverty in the world?

How should humankind treat the other species with which we share this planet? Should we eat them, destroy them by exploiting their natural environment, or try to protect them? Is it right to keep them as pets, or watch them in zoos?

This boy, sitting outside a hospital with a bowl of peanuts, is suffering from malnutrition and tuberculosis. In many countries, the problems of poverty and homelessness are made worse by political instability and civil war. (Mozambique; 1988)

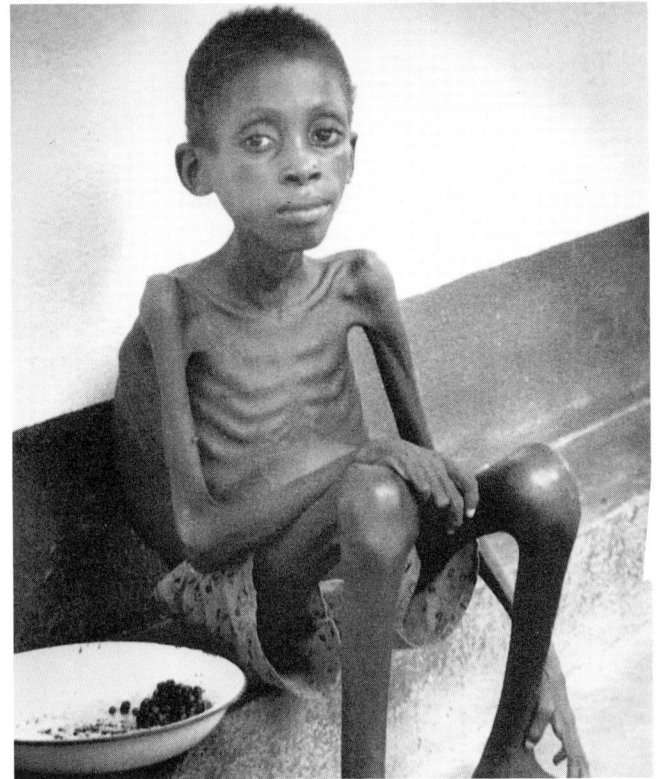

■ **Racism** and **women's rights** – *neither of these important issues is examined separately. The guidelines for these may be found in sections concerned with political action and human rights, and (in the case of women) in the sections on marriage and the family.*

■ **Wealth** – *This issue is generally covered in the third group, although not listed separately. The guidelines for wealth are connected with those for work and leisure, and with sharing resources with those who live in poverty.*

Issues are not listed in exactly the same way, nor dealt with at equal length, in all of the sections. This is because each religion emphasises certain guidelines more than others, and the overall balance of each section is designed to reflect this.

Judaism

THE TORAH

Central to the Jewish guidelines for life is the *Torah*, which means 'Teaching' or 'Law'. This refers to the first five books of the Jewish Bible (called the Old Testament in a Christian Bible), but for a Jew it means far more than the rules that are given there. Jews believe that the *Torah* was given by God to Moses, but that it existed before the creation of the world. *Torah* is described as the blueprint of creation, the wisdom and reason which form the basis of everything, and without which Heaven and Earth would not exist.

Jews believe that the *Torah* is like a harmonious pulse that goes through all creation, but that it is expressed for them in terms of a system of laws and rituals by means of which they can live as God intends.

The most famous of these laws are the Ten Commandments (Exodus 20: 1–17), which, in a shortened form, are:

1 I am the Lord your God.
2 You shall have no other God.
3 You shall not misuse God's name.
4 Remember to keep the Sabbath day holy.
5 Honour your father and your mother.
6 You shall not commit murder.
7 You shall not commit adultery.
8 You shall not steal.
9 You shall not give false evidence against your neighbour.
10 You shall not envy anything of your neighbour's.

The *Torah* contains 603 other laws, covering ethical and social matters and the rules for performing religious rituals. It was summed up by Rabbi Hillel, who lived in the first century B.C.E., like this: What is hateful to you do not do to another: and Leviticus 19: 18, offers another summary: . . . love your neighbour as yourself.

The Jewish term for a commandment is *mitzvah*, and the ceremony at which a young Jewish person accepts responsibility for keeping the Jewish guidelines is therefore called Bar Mitzvah (Son of the Commandment) or Bat Mitzvah (Daughter of the Commandment). Jews regard the *Torah* as a privilege rather than a burden. Its rules are the means by which people can please God and live in peace with one another.

THE TALMUD

No legal system is unchanging. If it did not change, it would soon be out of date. Judaism realised this and kept the *Torah* laws relevant by constantly reinterpreting them in the light of new situations. These interpretations were passed on by word of mouth over the centuries and are believed to have been received by Moses from God along with the written *Torah*. They are known as the oral *Torah*.

Eventually, in about 200 C.E., these traditions were written down, in a book which is called the *Mishna*. In time, this too needed reinterpreting, so a commentary, called the *Gemara*, was added. The Mishnah and Gemara printed together form the **Talmud.** This is a complex encyclopaedia of religious rules and traditions, running to many volumes and completed in about 600 C.E.

All these detailed guidelines for life are intended to help Jews to keep the commandments. The right way to follow these is called the *halakah*, or 'path'.

- Why do you think Jews may want to say that the *Torah* existed before the creation of the world?

- Why do you think that the *Torah* needs so much interpretation?

PROGRESSIVE JUDAISM

Different Jewish communities interpret the rules of the *Torah* in different ways. Orthodox Jews claim that all law comes from heaven, whether written or part of oral tradition and it must therefore be followed in every detail. Progressive Jews, those belonging to the Reform and Liberal traditions, believe that the *Torah* was written over many centuries and by many different people. This means that not all *mitzvot* (commandments) are directly from God, or need to be followed in the same way. There is therefore great variety in the detailed interpretation of Jewish guidelines.

Social customs and styles of dress also vary considerably. These do not come from the *Torah*, but from the various societies in which Jews have found themselves.

> * Which do you believe is more important – to keep detailed rules or to take a more liberal interpretation of the Jewish guidelines? Try to relate your answer to the idea of *'halakah'*.

YOM KIPPUR

In theory, Jews should be able to live up to all the requirements of God's law, but in practice it is impossible because human nature is weak, and prone to temptation. Wrongdoing is seen as a barrier between people and God. **It is therefore important to express sorrow for failings, and to receive forgiveness and the assurance of a new start.** Jews do this at Yom Kippur (The Day of Atonement), which takes place soon after the start of the Jewish New Year. It is a time when Jews review their lives in the light of the guidelines given them in the *Torah*. It is also an opportunity for people to settle any disputes they have with one another, for only then will they feel able to ask for God's forgiveness. They fast for twenty-five hours, and spend most of the day in prayer.

THE TWO IMPULSES

Jews believe that people are created with two basic impulses; the one good (seen in reason and purposeful living) and the other bad (seen in desire and raw energy). Both are aspects of the human personality, but the power of the evil impulse should be harnessed to do what is good (e.g. anger or ambition can be controlled, in order to produce something worthwhile).

> * Can you think of another evil impulse which could be harnessed for good?

THIS WORLD AND THE NEXT

Jews believe that the world can be made perfect by all human beings acting in accordance with God's wishes. In particular, if all Jews observed all the commandments, the Messiah (a man specially chosen by God) would come and put an end to war, famine and illness.

Some Jews think that when the Messiah comes, all people who have died will be resurrected and judged by God according to their deeds. **But Jews should not do good in the hope of future reward. Their task is to banish evil in this world, rather than think of the next.**

SUMMARY OF JEWISH GUIDELINES

* *Keep the commandments of the* Torah *in the correct way, following the* halakah *('path').*
* *Guided by the Talmud, interpret the rules and apply them to your own situation.*
* *Control the evil impulse that is within you, and use its power for good.*

Over to you

1 Using a textbook on Judaism, look up the beliefs and values that are expressed in the Jewish observation of:
   Passover
   Yom Kippur
2 Make notes on the difference between Orthodox, Reform and Liberal Judaism. These differences influence the way in which the Jewish guidelines are applied.
3 In following the Torah, Jews are keeping their side of a Covenant (agreement) with God. Look up the Covenants between God and the Jews in a textbook on Judaism.

Marriage and the family

SEX

Sex within marriage is regarded by Jews as a good and natural thing. It is the duty of every Jewish male to marry and have a family, for in the account of creation in Genesis, men and women are told to be fruitful and increase in number. Noah is told the same thing after the flood (Genesis 9:1–7). It also says that it is not good for a man to be alone, giving this as the reason why Eve was created for Adam (Genesis 1:20–22). In the Talmud there is a saying
. . . without a wife, man is incomplete.

The *halakah* emphasises that a husband should be sexually considerate towards his wife. He should not force her to have intercourse and should try to give her pleasure. A Jewish couple may abstain from sex for a few days each month after the wife's period, after which she takes a special bath, to show that she is ritually clean and able to have sex again.

Sex outside marriage is condemned and in ancient Israel both partners would have been severely punished. Homosexuality is forbidden in the *Torah*.

There are many rules designed to prevent people from being tempted sexually. Unmarried men and women should not be together in a closed room or house. In business, men should not take a position of authority over women which would allow them to be familiar with women. Men are warned not to be close to women, gaze on their beauty, smell their perfume or walk behind them!

Naturally enough, few Jewish people observe all these rules, but in strict Orthodox communities boys and girls are brought up separately, and in Orthodox synagogues men and women sit apart.

These rules are not designed to frustrate sexual feelings, but to avoid situations in which people may be sexually tempted.

- Most of the guidelines about sex apply to men. How should women respond? What behaviour should they avoid?
- Do you think these rules are fair?

MARRIAGE

Polygamy (a man having more than one wife) occurs in the scriptures, although a king is warned not to have 'many' wives. But, for European Jews, this was banned in the eleventh century C.E. (at the Rabbinical Synod of Worms), and monogamy (having only one wife) had become the normal practice among the Jewish people long before that.

In some traditional Jewish communities, where unmarried boys and girls are kept apart, marriages may be arranged between families and there may be an engagement ceremony (called *Tenaim*) where payment of a dowry is agreed. Penalties for breaking the engagement are also settled and an earthenware plate is broken as a reminder of the destruction of the Temple in Jerusalem. In less strict Jewish circles, the choice of partner is made by the individuals, with a secular engagement party.

A Jewish Wedding ceremony involves three things:

1 The *Ketuba*
This is an agreement, drawn up before the wedding day, and signed during the ceremony. It states that the bride and groom agree to 'cherish, respect and support' one another. Orthodox Jews also include

details of the financial provisions that aim to give the bride security in case she is divorced or widowed, but progressive Jews no longer do so.

2 The *chuppah v' Kidushin*

The *chuppah* is the canopy under which the wedding ceremony is performed. *Kedushin* means 'made holy', and expresses God's blessing on the marriage. A woman is considered to be married from the moment the *ketuba* is signed, and she then steps under the canopy, which represents the marital home.

The ceremony is carried out by a person called the *messader kidushin*, who is usually a Rabbi. After blessings and the sharing of a cup of wine (which symbolises joy, and is used by Jews on every joyous occasion), the groom puts a ring on the bride's finger saying 'By this ring you are married to me in holiness according to the law of Moses and of Israel'. In Reform and Liberal synagogues, the bride may then repeat this for the groom.

At the end of the ceremony, the groom breaks a glass, another reminder of the destruction of the Temple in Jerusalem.

3 Living together

The couple must live together as man and wife for the marriage to be complete.

At the end of the religious ceremony, the couple sign the registers. This is not part of the ceremony itself, but is required by the civil law just as if they were in a registry office. Although unusual, it is possible for the couple to have a registry office wedding first, and then to go on to the religious service.

Because the marriage is conducted 'according to the law of Moses and Israel', it can only take place if both bride and groom are Jewish. A non-Jew wishing to marry a Jew must convert to Judaism first, if they are to have a religious wedding.

- Do you think it is wise for the *ketuba* to include financial arrangements in case of divorce? State your reasons.

PARENTHOOD AND FAMILY LIFE

Family life is an important part of Judaism, and children are considered to be a blessing.

The use of contraception is debated: some Jews think it is right, but only after having at least one son and one daughter. Most accept contraception if there is a risk to the health of the mother in having more children.

The Talmud gives this advice on care for wife and family:

> A man should spend less than his means on food and drink for himself, up to his means on clothes, and above his means on honouring his wife and children.

- What reason might a Jewish person give for saying that a large family is a blessing? Do you agree?

The most important time of the week for a Jewish family is when they gather together on a Friday evening for the Sabbath meal.

Sometimes different generations in a family live in the same house, or very near one another, forming what is called an 'extended' family. The help that they can give one another is an important part of Jewish family life. Where members of a family live apart, they may still gather together for the major festivals – particularly at New Year, and for the Sedar meal at Passover.

A Jewish family gather to celebrate Passover.

In Israel, there are communities of people who live and work together on what are called 'Kibbutzim'. Within each Kibbutz, property is held in common, and children generally live together with those of their own age, rather than with their families. Yet even on a Kibbutz, family life is seen as important, and children will spend Sabbaths and festivals with their parents.

ADULTERY AND DIVORCE

Deuteronomy 20:22, prescribes the death penalty for those who are guilty of adultery. This sort of punishment is not carried out in modern times, but it shows the seriousness with which Judaism views adultery. Deuteronomy 24:10 gives 'shameful conduct' as a reason for divorce. Some Rabbis interpreted this to mean adultery, but others thought it could be extended to cover other things as well.

Since marriage is a voluntary agreement between two people, divorce is allowed. The term used for a divorce is *Get* (there is a section of the Talmud called *Gittin* which deals with this, just as there is one called *Ketubot*, for marriage). A court of three rabbis, called a *Bet Din* prepares the divorce document, usually at the request of the husband (although a wife can apply for divorce) and this is then delivered to the other partner.

A wife may divorce her husband if she can show that he is: unfaithful; sterile; impotent; depriving her of money to live on; cruel; or irreligious.

Except in Israel, where a husband can be imprisoned if he refuses to divorce his wife, a husband is not bound to accept the ruling of the *Bet Din*. If he does not give her a *get*, she is not allowed to remarry.

In any case, the divorced wife is not allowed to remarry for three months after a *get*, in order to establish that she is not pregnant by the former husband. Orthodox Jews would consider a child illegitimate unless a woman had a legal *get* document, showing that she was married at the time of conception.

A child who is considered illegitimate according to Jewish law, is called a *mamzer*, and is only allowed to marry another *mamzer* or a convert to Judaism. It is therefore important for a woman to make sure she has a *get* document.

Although Western Jews generally do not allow a husband to divorce his wife against her will, in many other ways, as shown above, men have an advantage over women when it comes to divorce. In particular, women find it difficult to start divorce proceedings and courts try to keep families together. Because of this, Reform Jews have their own *get* which treats husband and wife equally, and Liberal Jews can now do without religious divorce altogether.

Divorce is seen as a serious and sad event, and in the *Gittin* section of the Talmud it says:

> If a man divorces his first wife – even the altar (of the Temple) sheds tears.

- Do you think that the traditional Jewish guidelines on divorce are fair to women?
- Do you agree with the grounds on which a wife may ask for a divorce?
- Do you think it is right for a man to be compelled to divorce his wife, if they are separated and she wants to remarry?

CARE OF THE ELDERLY

Honouring your father and mother is the only one of the Ten Commandments which has a promise attached to it – that you yourself may enjoy a long life. Proverbs 23:22 says:

> Listen to your father, who gave you life,
>   and do not despise your mother when she is old.

Jewish families therefore see it as a religious responsibility to take care of their elderly parents and other relatives. If a parent becomes senile, or for some other reason cannot be cared for at home, his or her children still have a responsibility to see that proper care is provided. Wisdom is associated with old age, so the older a person is, the greater the respect in which he or she is held.

ABORTION AND EUTHANASIA

Generally speaking, the Jewish religion prohibits the taking of life at any time from the moment of conception to that of natural death. In the case of euthanasia, Judaism will allow nothing that hastens death in any way.

This prohibition applies to abortion, except in certain circumstances. **A Jewish person is allowed to kill in self defence.** Therefore, it is permitted to carry out an abortion if the foetus threatens the life of the mother. Some Rabbis would add that it may be permitted if the birth of the child is likely to lead the mother to despair or suicide, or if (e.g. through extreme poverty or overcrowding, her mental health may be affected). When does a foetus become an individual with rights? Most Jewish authorities say that this happens at the moment of birth, because, until that moment, the unborn baby is not independent of its mother. This means that the unborn child may be sacrificed for the sake of the mother's life, up until the moment of birth, but from then on mother and baby have equal rights.

In order to avoid unnecessary suffering, many Rabbis would accept that abortion is possible if a child is likely to be born severely deformed; and, in this case, it should be performed as early as possible in pregnancy.

- Do you think that a foetus becomes a child with individual rights only at the moment of birth?
- Do you agree with these Jewish guidelines about when abortion is permitted?

Over to you

1 Using a textbook on Judaism, note down the way in which Jewish people observe the Sabbath. Then list those ways in which the Sabbath may influence family life and relationships.
2 Look up the differences between Sephardi and Ashkenazi Jews. Look up the areas and cultures among which each group has lived, and then suggest why Sephardi Jews have sometimes continued to practise polygamy. (Clue: With which other religions would the Sephardim come into contact?)

Peace and conflict

Jews greet one another with the word *Shalom*, meaning 'peace', and there is a hope (expressed in Isaiah 2:4) that ultimately nations will beat their swords into ploughshares and war will become a thing of the past. Jewish guidelines for dealing with violence and war must therefore be seen against the background of this hope for peace.

INDIVIDUAL VIOLENCE

The Jewish guideline on this is that you should not act violently, nor kill another person, except in self-defence.

There is a tradition which says:

He who rises up to slay you, rise up and slay him first.

If your own life is in danger, you may kill an attacker, but you should not kill an innocent person, even if it is in order to save your own life. This comes from the idea that, of the 613 commandments of the *Torah*, 610 of them may be broken in order to save your own life. The three exceptions are: murder; sexual immorality; and idolatry.

Even in the case of self-defence, some Jews find the use of violence something which they feel to be wrong.

In Israel, where young Jews are required to serve in the army, some find that any violent action they have to take troubles their conscience. Others justify violence by saying that evil must be prevented, whatever the cost. Others feel that they should use only sufficient force to defend themselves.

Since the Holocaust – when six million Jews were killed by the Nazis during the Second World War – Jews have been specially aware of the need for self-defence and the importance of opposing evil.

- How might a person use the Jewish guidelines given above to justify violent action taken against those who are involved in a riot, or who are thought to be terrorists?
- When do you think it is right to defend yourself by using force – when your life is threatened, or when you think there is a chance of being hurt?

CAPITAL PUNISHMENT

Jewish guidelines permit capital punishment for serious offences. Leviticus 24:17 says:

"If anyone takes the life of a human being, he must be put to death . . ."

In the same passage in Leviticus, best known for the expression 'an eye for an eye', the important thing is that **punishment should be restrained** and should never exceed the original crime. The idea of taking unlimited revenge on a person who has done wrong, is condemned.

In the Talmud, there are two conditions that make it possible to sentence a murderer to death:

1 The murderer must have been warned about the consequences of his or her action twice before committing the crime.
2 There must be two independent witnesses to the murder.

In practice, this meant that very few murderers could be given the death sentence and that it would be impossible for an innocent person to be executed by mistake.

17

The Talmud also has a rule that a convicted criminal should be given wine and a drug before being executed. This is so that the person may lose consciousness and not suffer a painful death. **Capital punishment, if it is to be carried out, must be done in a humane way.**

- Do you approve of the restrictions the Talmud places on capital punishment?

MINORITY RIGHTS

Jews have suffered as a result of being a minority group as they have always been easily identified by their appearance and way of life within the different countries where they have lived. They therefore tend to give their support to other minority groups.

Only in modern Israel do Jews find themselves as the majority group in society. Yet in Israel, Jews are still confronted with the problems of minority rights because there is a minority of Arabs living in Israel.

There is also concern about the Palestinian Arabs who live in those areas which are outside Israel itself, but which are controlled by the Israeli army. In these 'occupied territories' there are both Arab and Jewish settlements. There is tension between these groups and frequent acts of violence, protesting against the presence of the Israeli army.

In 1988, Israel's Supreme Court, claiming to defend the standards of the founding fathers of Israel, upheld the ban on the Kach Party. Kach is a political group led by Rabbi Meir Kahane, which the court decided was racist, inciting hatred between Jews and non-Jews. Kach wants to expel Arabs from Israel, expanding the country to include the 'occupied territory' of the West Bank. This court decision upheld Israel's 1985 legislation against the promotion of racism.

A Palestinian woman tries to prevent Israeli soldiers from arresting an Arab youth. (Bethlehem; July 1989)

The protection of minority groups follows directly from the *Torah*, where the alien is to be treated with compassion, just like the poor people within Israel.

- In what ways do you think the experience of being a persecuted minority has influenced the Jewish attitude towards the Palestinian Arabs who live in Israel and the 'occupied territories'?

SECULAR AUTHORITY

In the period before and during the Second World War, Jews suffered persecution by the secular authorities in Nazi Germany and in those countries (particularly Poland) occupied by the Germans. Six million Jews died as a result of a deliberate policy of extermination, in what is known as 'The Holocaust'.

This event, more than any other in modern times, shows the threat that can be posed by secular political authorities to people of a particular religious and cultural group.

Anatoly Sharansky

Jewish people accept the secular laws of the country within which they live, but, since they also belong to the Jewish community, they need to make special provisions to enable them to follow their religious guidelines as well.

Where the secular authorities go against their convictions about religious and human rights, Jews may campaign for the laws to be changed. For example, in the Soviet Union, some Jews have been refused permission to emigrate to Israel. They are sometimes referred to as 'refuseniks'. Others have campaigned on their behalf and in favour of the implementation of basic human rights.

Those who campaign in this way are known as 'dissidents'. One of the best known of these is Anatoly Sharansky, who spent many years in prison and labour camp, experienced systemic ill treatment and went on hunger strike, before he was finally expelled from the Soviet Union in 1986.

- Is there anything about which you feel strongly enough that you would want to campaign for it, against the laws of the country in which you live?

- How do you think secular authorities should deal with those who campaign against them?

WARFARE

The Jewish scriptures record the struggle of the tribes of Israel to establish themselves in Palestine. Later they were to suffer defeat at the hands of the Assyrian, Babylonian, Greek and Roman empires, so for one thousand nine hundred years there was no Jewish state.

Since the modern state of Israel was established, there have been five wars:

1 The War of Independence (1948/49)
2 The Sinai Campaign (1956)
3 The Six-Day War (1967)
4 The War of Attrition (1969–70)
5 The Yom Kippur War (1973)

More recently, Jewish troops have been involved in the Lebanon, taking action against Palestinian groups thought to be responsible for terrorist attacks against Israel.

Alongside these major periods of conflict, Israel has responded to terrorist attacks and during 1988 and 1989 Israeli troops were involved in containing an uprising by Palestinian Arabs in the 'occupied territories' of the West Bank and Gaza Strip.

Although Israel is a secular state (that is, it is not organised on religious principles), almost all its soldiers are Jewish. Jews are therefore involved today in the issues of war and peace.

The guideline used for warfare is the same as for individual acts of violence. **Force should only be used in self defence, or in order to prevent an attack taking place.** This last rule means that armed forces are justified in attacking any target which poses a serious threat to the nation's security.

No one should kill or wound a person in war out of a desire to inflict pain or as an act of revenge, but only in order to control a situation in order to prevent further violence, and with the hope of restoring peace – *Shalom*.

- In what circumstances do you think it is reasonable to attack an enemy as a means of self-defence?

The remains of the fortress at Masada.

In 70 C.E. the Romans captured Jerusalem and destroyed the Temple. Nearly a thousand Jewish rebels, men women and children, held out in the desert fortress of Masada and late in 72 C.E. a force of between ten and fifteen thousand Romans laid seige to it.

When the Romans were about to break in and the situation was seen to be hopeless, the rebels decided to destroy all their goods and then commit suicide, rather than be captured by the Romans.

Although suicide is seen as murder, and is therefore condemned by Jewish law, the determination of the defenders of Masada to remain free is seen as an example of courage in the face of an evil enemy.

This suggests two further guidelines. The first is that **death is better than slavery**, and the second (sometimes expressed in the saying 'Masada shall not fall again!'), is that **Jews will fight to defend their claim to the land of Israel**.

The Jewish festival of Channukah, recalls the cleansing of the Temple in Jerusalem of the images that had been set up in it during a period of Greek domination. This cleansing was made possible by a revolt against the Greek rulers, led by a family called the Maccabees. Their aim was to restore the Jewish traditions of life and worship.

- Do you think it is right to go to war only to defend religious principles (like the Maccabees) and not when you are physically threatened by an enemy?

Over to you

1 Imagine that you are in charge of a military operation. You have identified a camp where the enemy are in training and where they have a store of weapons. You cannot approach the camp openly without putting your troops at risk. Outline the dilemmas you face if you apply the Jewish guidelines for warfare and violence to that situation. What would be your decision, following those guidelines? Would you, personally, agree with it?
2 Collect articles from the newspapers about the situation in the Middle East, particularly those which give details of incidents in which the Israeli army is involved. Then, using the guidelines in this section, evaluate the moral dilemmas a Jew faces in that situation.

Humankind and nature

REVERENCE FOR LIFE

Judaism teaches that **all life should be treated with respect, since it has been created by God**. This is especially true of human life, which Jews believe to have been formed in God's own image.

Because life is precious, Jewish guidelines say that you should never stand by and allow someone to die if there is any way in which you can save his or her life, even if it involves breaking religious rules (e.g. by working on a Sabbath, or by offering food which is normally forbidden to Jews).

Generally speaking, Jews take the view that a person should treat his or her own body with care and that a person should not deny himself or herself any legitimate pleasure. In Judaism the body is not thought of as evil, for although everyone has evil impulses, these can be channelled for good.

This respect for the human body means that Jews should not harm it through the misuse of drugs or excessive alcohol. It also means that a person is obliged to get medical help for himself or herself in the case of illness.

Unless it is done for a specific purpose, there is no benefit to be gained from self-denial.

THE ENVIRONMENT

Jews believe that when God had finished creating the world, he looked at everything and it was good (Genesis 1:31). **Humankind does not own the world, but has been given authority over it (Genesis 1:26), as a steward, responsible to God for the way in which it is treated.**

In the Jewish scriptures there are practical guidelines for the maintenance of the environment. In Exodus 23:10 the land is to lay fallow for one year in seven. This is partly to help the poor, who may gather whatever grows on it, but it also enables the land to rest and renew itself. In Deuteronomy 20:19, 22:6, even in a time of war, fruit trees are not to be cut down in a seige. This is so that, when peace returns, people can resume their normal life on the land.

This guideline is reinforced by a sense of religious wonder. Psalm 19 expresses the idea that the heavens declare God's glory. The natural order is seen as a pointer to God, and must therefore be treated with respect.

- What is the difference between a steward and an owner? How does this affect the Jewish attitude towards the environment?

WORK AND LEISURE

In Genesis, God is said to have worked at creation for six days and then rested on the seventh. So too Jews are expected to engage in work, except on the Sabbath.

Jews believe that a person is not fully human without some creative work to do. It is a means of expressing human personality, and is believed to be the way in which humankind shares in the work of God.

Ideally, work should not be a burden, but something enjoyable and it is important that everyone takes a fair share in it:

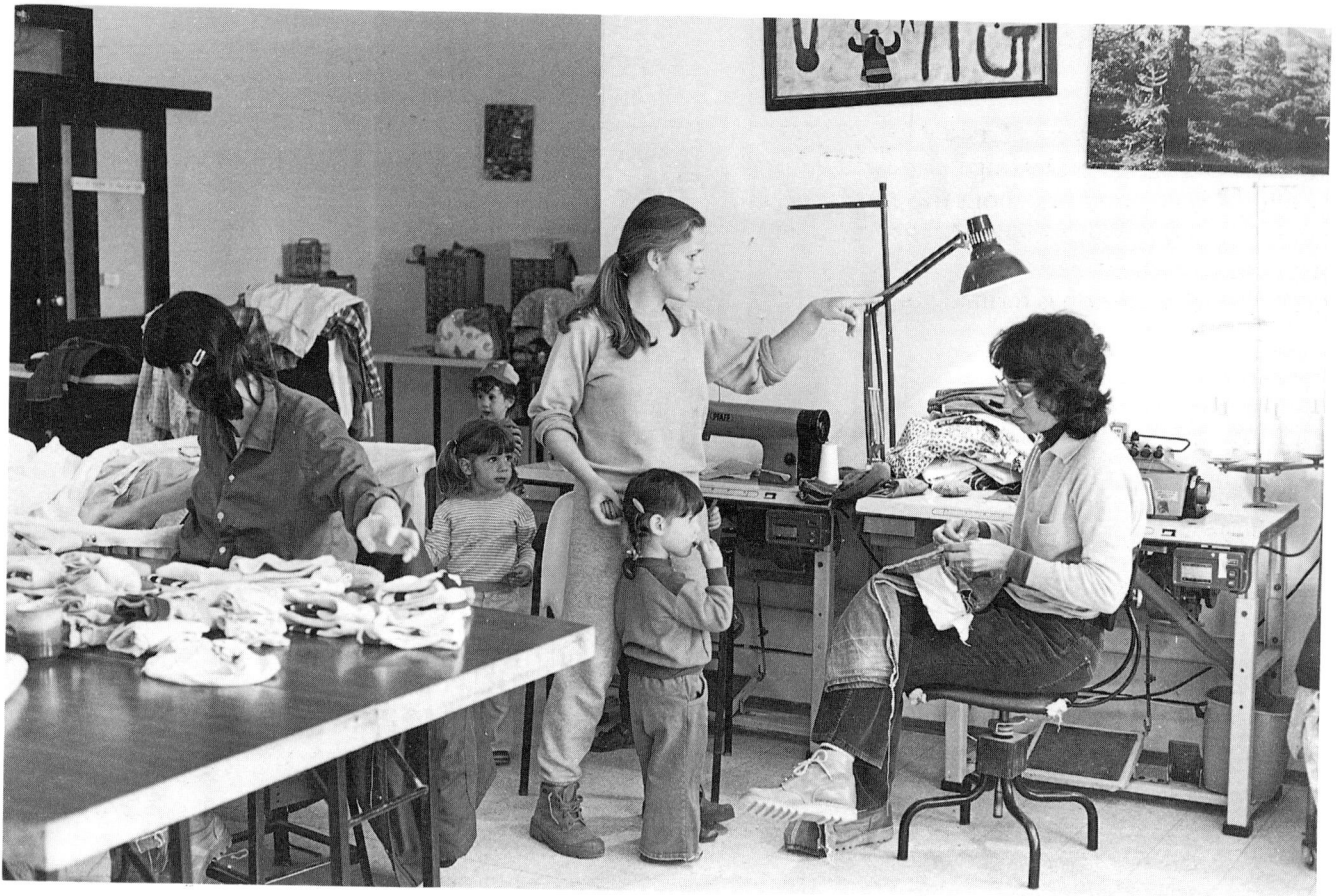

Working together: children from the kindergarten visit the laundry at Kerem Shalom Kibbutz in Israel.

One who is slack in his work
　　is brother to one who destroys.　　　　(Proverbs 18:9)

A similar view is expressed in the Talmud:

He who does not teach his son a trade is as though he taught him to be a robber.

The Jewish teacher Gamaliel set down this principle:

Excellent is the study of the Torah combined with a worldly occupation for the toil involved in both makes sin to be forgotten.

Therefore, although the study of the *Torah* may be the most important activity for a Jew, it should be combined with practical work.

Those who employ others should be fair in their dealings with them, and Deuteronomy 24:15 insists that wages should be paid promptly, so that working people should not remain in need.

Work should bring spiritual and moral benefit, as well as contributing to society. But money earned should not be hoarded for its own sake. The author of Ecclesiastes 5:10 warns:

Whoever loves money never has money enough;
　　Whoever loves wealth is never satisfied with his income.
　　This too is meaningless.

On the other hand, Jews argue that, if people did nothing but work, they would be little more than robots. Therefore, leisure is more important than work, and by observing the Sabbath, Jews have made space in their lives for rest and leisure activities. Family life, friendships and religion would all be threatened if there were no time for leisure.

- What creative work do you do? Do you enjoy it?

- Do you think it is easier to express your personality through work or through leisure? Give your reasons. Can you think of anyone for whom the opposite answer would be true?

FOOD AND DRINK

The Jewish religion is concerned with every aspect of life, and Jews say a blessing before eating or drinking. There are rules about the preparation of food, and about which foods may be eaten. Food and drink which is selected and prepared according to the Jewish tradition is termed *kosher*.

Most Jews eat meat, but the animal must be killed in the correct way (by cutting its throat as quickly and humanely as possible and by making sure that all the blood has drained from the body before the meat is cooked). Some animals (e.g. pigs) and some seafood are not *kosher*.

Some rabbis argue that humankind did not eat meat before the Flood (animals were only offered as sacrifices to God) and that when Noah was allowed meat, it was as a concession to human desires and was to be eaten in moderation. They therefore claim that the Jewish moral law should point towards vegetarianism.

FASTING

At certain times, Jewish people go without food, as part of their spiritual discipline, and to show sorrow for their sins. Yom Kippur (The Day of Atonement) is one such day.

The rules about food and fasting are less important than caring for those in need. Therefore, those who are young, infirm or elderly, do not need to keep to a fast if it might harm them to do so.

The Talmud advises that, if a person is ill and it is necessary for recovery he or she eats a forbidden food, then that person should be allowed to have it. Also, when on a fast, a person may be given food (even forbidden food, if nothing else is available) if he or she feels faint and ravenously hungry. These rules illustrate the general guideline, that **rules about food and religious duties must take second place to showing mercy and saving life.**

- Why do you think it is appropriate for Jews to fast on Yom Kippur? (To answer this, you may need to refer back to the section on Yom Kippur in the general guidelines.)

HELPING THE POOR

In the Jewish scriptures there are many rules which try to ensure that the poor are given a share of the food that the land produces, and that those who are slaves or who are in debt have some chance of making a better life for themselves.

But should you be prepared to share everything in order to save the life of those who are desperately in need? In the Talmud, the dilemma is posed like this:

Imagine two people in the desert with a supply of water sufficient for only one of them. What should you do in such circumstances?

The scholars disagreed. Ben Peturah advocated that neither should try to save his own life at the expense of the other, but that they should share the water. Avika argued that a person had a duty to save his or her life and that each would therefore be justified if he took the water. Offering up one's life, he said, was only to be preferred if the alternative involved committing idolatry, having unlawful sexual intercourse, committing murder, or renouncing your faith in public. In all other circumstances you should save yourself.

- Do you agree with Ben Peturah or Akiva? What would you do in those circumstances?

Other laws ensure that the natural resources of the Earth are shared out with those who do not own them. In Exodus 23:11, a person may gather crops from the land for six years, but on the seventh year the land is to lie unploughed and unused. This is so that the poor may get food from it and so that wild animals may eat what the poor leave. In Leviticus 19:9, 10 a farmer is instructed not to reap right up to the edges of his field, gather the gleanings of the harvest, or go over a vineyard a second time to pick up the grapes that have fallen. These are all to be left for the benefit of the poor and the alien.

Where rich people are condemned by the prophets in ancient Israel, it was not because their wealth was bad in itself, but because they failed to share it with the poor.

In Rabbinic literature, the word used for charity is *Zedakah*. This means 'justice' and suggests that giving to the poor is not a favour that is done for them, but is what God requires, and an obligation on the giver.

Everyone is required to give charity. Even a person who receives charity should give some of it to a person less fortunate. In distributing charity, the principle set down by the rabbis was that women should come before men, and one's own relatives before strangers.

One-tenth of a person's income is regarded as an acceptable amount to give to charity. Ideally the charity should be given in such a way that the giver and the receiver do not know one another. Nothing should be done which might make the recipient feel ashamed.

In *Jewish Values*, Maimonides lists eight ways of giving charity, each one better than the last:

1 to give sadly;
2 to give less than is suitable, but cheerfully;
3 to give only after having been asked;
4 to give before being asked;
5 to give in such a way that the recipient does not know who gave it;
6 to give in such a way that neither knows who the other is;
7 not to give charity, but to take the poor into business partnerships or lend them money so that they can improve their situation without any loss of self-respect.

- How might the principles laid down by Maimonides be applied to the work of charities involved with development aid? What should their aim be?

ANIMALS

Because they are believed to be part of God's creation, **Judaism requires compassion to be shown towards animals.**

Rules about the Sabbath apply to domestic animals as well as to humans (see Exodus 20:10), so that they too may have a time of rest.

When animals are to be slaughtered, the killing is done by a *shochet* (slaughterer), who is specially trained to do it as quickly and painlessly as possible.

Judaism does not approve of hunting animals (not even for a living) and there is a Rabbinic rule that one should not buy any animal unless you can properly provide for it.

The rabbis also argued that unnecessary pain should never be inflicted on an animal, and that it was wrong to blemish or injure it in any way. Even where some pain is unavoidable, this is still seen as cruel.

- How might these guidelines be applied to the use of animals in scientific experiments or to farming methods?

Over to you

1 Read Psalm 8. In what way does this illustrate the Jewish guidelines for dealing with nature?
2 Try to find out about life on the Kibbutzim in Israel. Note down ways in which they reflect the Jewish attitudes to work, leisure and the community.

Christianity

Christian guidelines for life are based on the teaching and example of Jesus of Nazareth. But Christians do not always agree about how they should interpret that teaching or apply it to present-day situations. How do they decide what is right?

AUTHORITY

Some Christians (particularly those who belong to the Protestant churches) argue that the only authority for deciding Christian guidelines is **the Bible**. Some take every word of it literally, and give each passage an equal authority. Others point out that the Bible contains many different kinds of writing – poetry; myth (a story which is made up in order to express an important religious truth); history; and teachings. Each of these needs to be interpreted differently. Even the teachings of Jesus (e.g. in The Sermon on the Mount, Matthew 5–7) were not written down until many years after his death, but were originally passed on by word of mouth. We may not therefore be certain that we know exactly the words that Jesus used. Those who take the Bible as the authority for what is right or wrong, need to interpret it carefully in order to understand its meaning for Christians today.

Other Christians emphasise **the Church and its teachings** as the authority for understanding right and wrong. They argue that God's Holy Spirit inspires the Church (the whole community of Christians) and enables it to interpret and apply Jesus' teaching correctly. Roman Catholic Christians accept the special authority of **the Pope (the Bishop of Rome)**. They claim that, when he makes an official statement on a matter of faith or morals, with the full authority of his position as head of the Catholic Church, they accept that what he says must be correct.

Christians believe that God created the world and that he gave to it a sense of order and purpose. They may therefore argue that **human reason**, as it studies the laws of nature, should offer guidelines for understanding right from wrong. If everything has its own natural purpose in life, then human reason can understand that if something is unnatural, then it is wrong.

When Christians face a difficult decision and they do not find a clear answer from the Bible or the teachings of the Church, they may **pray to God for guidance**. As a result of this prayer, they may then be convinced about what is right for them. A person's **conscience** may also suggest that a particular action is wrong, and he or she may believe that God is speaking through the voice of his or her conscience.

- The Bible; the Church; reason; prayer; conscience.
  List these in order of importance you think they should have for Christian guidelines for life, giving your reasons.

KEEPING THE RULES?

Jesus was a Jew. He did not put aside the moral and religious rules of the Jewish people, but claimed that he was fulfilling and completing them.

Christians therefore accept the Jewish moral guidelines (e.g. the Ten Commandments) and use the Jewish scriptures (which they call The Old Testament), but they claim to go **beyond the Law**, by considering attitude as well as action.

For example, the Jewish Law condemned murder and adultery, but Jesus went beyond this and said that a person who hated someone without a cause was guilty of murder and one who looked at someone with feelings of lust was guilty of adultery. In other words, **it is not just the action, but the thought of it that makes a person guilty in the sight of God.**

- If thinking something is as bad as doing it, why not just go ahead and do whatever you want?
- Do you think Jesus meant people to take this teaching literally?
- How might this influence your view of a person who has committed murder or adultery?

SIN AND FORGIVENESS

'Sin' means separation from God, caused by a person's failure to live up to what God wants. Christians believe that, since nobody is perfect, everyone is guilty of sin and needs forgiveness. They believe that their sin is forgiven by God, without them having done anything to earn that forgiveness. This is called 'grace' – something freely given.

But sin also separates people from one another. In the Sermon on the Mount, Jesus said:

"... For if you forgive men when they sin against you, your heavenly Father will also forgive you. But if you do not forgive men their sins, your Father will not forgive your sins ..."

(Matthew 6:14, 15)

Forgiveness is therefore an important guideline for Christians. They do not claim to be morally superior to other people, but recognise that everyone needs to forgive and to be forgiven.

- Look up the parable of the Prodigal Son (Luke 15:11–32). What features of Jesus' teaching and ministry do you think it expresses?

LOVE

The Gospels describe Jesus healing the sick and accepting those people who were generally rejected by the society of his day.

Christians believe that Jesus' concern for people, expresses God's love for them. They also believe that they are given the power to love other people, because they first know themselves to be loved by God. In John's gospel, Jesus says:

"My command is this: Love each other as I have loved you ...

(John 15:12)

Love – not simply an emotion, but a concern and respect for people – is therefore the central Christian guideline and the person who loves is said to know God (1 John 4:8). The other qualities of the Christian life are seen as responses to God's love, rather than as personal achievements.

- Jesus taught that people should love their enemies. What might this mean in practice? Can you love someone without actually liking them?

SUMMARY OF CHRISTIAN GUIDELINES

- *Follow the teaching and example of Jesus, as these are recorded in the Bible and interpreted by the Church.*
- *Attitudes are important, as well as actions.*
- *Accept forgiveness, and be prepared to forgive others.*
- *Respond to God's love by loving others.*
- *Do not go against what your conscience tells you is right.*

Over to you

1 Look up the three main branches of the Christian Church (Orthodox, Roman Catholic and Protestant) in the textbook. Notice the kind of authority (e.g. of priests and bishops; of tradition; of Bible reading and preaching) that each claims for the way in which it presents Christian beliefs and guidelines.
2 Read Romans 12:1–15:6 and list the rules given there for life in the Christian community.
3 Read Galatians 5:16–26 and make two lists, one showing the qualities of sinful nature, the other showing those of the Spirit.

Marriage and the family

SEX AND CELIBACY

Christianity has many positive things to say about sexual intercourse within marriage. **It is seen as the means of working with God to produce new life and a way in which a couple may deepen their love for one another.**

Many Christians regard all sex outside marriage as sinful. Others may argue that sex should take place only in a relationship of love and trust (and therefore that sex might be wrong within a loveless marriage and right in a loving and stable relationship outside marriage). A minority of Christians would accept that a homosexual relationship is morally right, provided that it is an expression of love; but most Christians, following Romans 1:26, 27, say that homosexual acts are always wrong.

- Do you think it is morally right for *any* relationship to express itself sexually, provided that it is based on mutual love and trust, or should sex be reserved for marriage?

Some Christians remain celibate (that is, they live without a sexual relationship) for religious reasons. There are monks and nuns who live in religious communities and in the Roman Catholic tradition, priests are not allowed to marry. In the Orthodox Churches, although married men become parish priests, all senior positions in the Churches are held by those who have been monks and are therefore unmarried.

This does not mean that sex is wrong in itself, but that certain people have a vocation to serve the Church in a particular way, which requires them to do without sexual relationships.

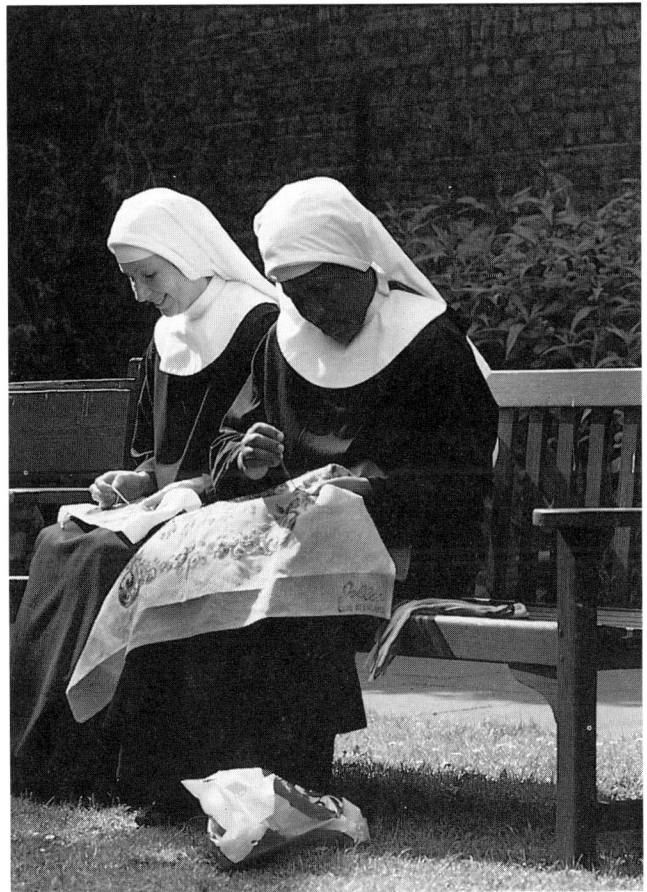

Monks and nuns have chosen to do without sex and family life for the sake of serving God in a special way. This does not mean that sex is bad, not that they are spiritually superior for having given it up.

MARRIAGE

Orthodox, Roman Catholic and some Protestant Christians regard marriage as a sacrament (a Mystery in the Orthodox tradition) which means that it is a special means by which God acts in people's lives. **All Christians see marriage as an expression of the love of God.**

Generally speaking, Christians choose their own marriage partners, with less parental involvement than is customary among other religious communities.

A couple become engaged to be married without any religious ceremony, but before a wedding can take place, they must either get a licence to marry from a registrar, or else they must have banns read out in a Church. The reading of banns takes place on three consecutive Sundays, during a service and gives people an opportunity to say if they know any legal reason why the couple cannot be married.

Guidelines for marriage are given in this introduction to a marriage service in the Anglican Church:

Marriage is given, that husband and wife may comfort and help each other, living faithfully together in need and in plenty, in sorrow and in joy. It is given, that with delight and tenderness they may know each other in love, and, through the joy of their bodily union, may strengthen the union of their hearts and lives

and that

they may have children and be blessed in caring for them and bringing them up in accordance with God's will . . .
(Alternative Service Book, 1980)

It also says that the couple should enter into marriage reverently, responsibly and after serious thought' rather than 'carelessly, lightly or selfishly'.

- What do you think is the biggest difficulty a young couple might find in trying to live up to these guidelines?

In the service, the couple may be asked:

Will you love her/him, comfort her/him, honour and protect her/him, and, forsaking all others, be faithful to her/him as long as you both shall live?

They then make promises to one another.

I (name), take you (name),
to be my wife/husband,
to have and to hold
from this day forward;
for better, for worse,
for richer, for poorer,
in sickness and in health,
to love and to cherish,
till death us do part,
according to God's holy law;
and this is my solemn vow.
(Alternative Service Book 1980)

(Other Christian denominations (e.g. Roman Catholic; Methodist) use different forms of words, but the basic guidelines remain the same.)

- In an alternative form of these vows, the man promises 'to love, cherish, and worship' his future wife, while she promises 'to love, cherish, and obey' him.
- What do you think worship means here?
- Do you think a wife should 'obey' her husband? Give your reasons?

In the Christian marriage ceremony, there is no formal contract setting out financial arrangements between the couple, but as they give and receive rings, they may promise:

. . . all that I am, I give to you,
and all that I have I share with you . . .

Most Christian traditions have three parts to a wedding service:

1 vows are exchanged
2 the man gives his bride a ring (or the couple exchange rings)
3 they join hands and receive a blessing.
In some Christian groups (e.g. the Society of Friends) the service may be very simple: the couple make a brief statement, declaring that they accept one another in marriage, in the presence of the church community.

- Do you think it would be an advantage or a disadvantage to have a written contract, or financial arrangements for the marriage, agreed at the time of the wedding?

A couple exchange rings at a Catholic wedding service. Rings are exchanged in most Christian traditions, as an expression and a reminder of the promises the couple make to one another.

PARENTHOOD

One of the reasons for marriage, according to the Christian guidelines, is that the couple should have children and bring them up in a home which offers love and security. Christians may describe having a family as sharing in God's work of creation.

Some Christians (particularly Roman Catholics) think that contraception is wrong. *Humanae Vitae*, an Encyclical Letter of Pope Paul VI (1968), argues that every sexual act should have the possibility of creating new life. It says that this is the natural function of sex and that contraception could lead to a lowering of moral standards and more temptation for couples to be unfaithful to one another. Because they see it as unnatural, Catholics also disapprove of any artificial methods of conception for naturally infertile couples.

Other Christians welcome family planning, in the hope that parents will only have children when they can provide for them properly, both economically and emotionally.

- Do you think that efficient contraception increases the risk of unfaithfulness?

Some Christian couples, whether or not they have children of their own, feel that they have a vocation to share their family life with other children, either through adoption of fostering. Rules for adopting and fostering children are not religious, but are part of the civil law.

DIVORCE

According to Mark 10:2–12, Jesus contrasted his view of marriage, with that of the Law of Moses, which allowed a man to divorce his wife. He argued that, from the creation, God intended men and women to be united in marriage. People should not separate what God had joined together. To divorce and remarry was therefore the equivalent of committing adultery. **This emphasises the ideal of marriage – which is faithfulness for life – and the seriousness of divorce.**

In interpreting it, we may need to consider two other Christian guidelines:

1 Jesus said that to look at another person with feelings of sexual lust was the equivalent of adultery. Therefore almost everyone shares in the feelings that lead to adultery, or the situation of a divorced person who wants to remarry.
2 Christians are required to show love and forgiveness towards others, no matter what they have done.

- How might these guidelines influence the Christian attitude to those who are divorced?

St Paul said that a wife should not separate from her husband, but, if she did, she should then remain unmarried (see 1 Corinthians 7:10, 11).

- Some denominations, including the Orthodox Churches, recognise divorce and will allow remarriage.
- The Methodist Church leaves the decision on remarriage to the individual minister.
- Some Churches will not allow a divorced person to remarry in Church, since it would involve taking lifelong vows for a second time, but will offer a service of blessing, following a marriage in a Registry Office.
- In exceptional circumstances, the Church of England will remarry divorced people, but only after their situation has been examined carefully,

and special permission is given by a bishop.
— The Roman Catholic Church does not accept divorce, but will sometimes annul a marriage (that is, they will say that it was never a proper marriage) if it is found that there was something wrong when a couple married, which, had they known it at the time, would have prevented them marrying.

Grounds for annulment include:
● a partner not being mature enough to enter into marriage;
● a partner not knowing that marriage is for life;
● a partner forced or frightened into marriage;
● nervous disorder or insanity at the time of marriage;
● impotence, where the marriage has not included a full sexual relationship between the partners;
● one or both partners making vows with no real intention of keeping them.
   After annulment, the partners are free to marry.

● Do you think a couple ever know one another well enough to take the marriage vows without some doubt in their minds?

ABORTION

A majority of Christians (particularly Catholics) regard the killing of an unborn child as morally wrong. Catholics hold that a foetus has the same right to life as its mother (Encyclical *Casti Conubii*: Pius XII; 1930).
   Others say that a foetus may be aborted if it is seriously deformed, if the mother's life is put in danger by continuing with the pregnancy, or following rape.
   Christians may argue that it is better for a child to be adopted, if its mother cannot care for it herself, rather than have it aborted. No two situations are exactly alike, and **most Christians will try to balance the rights of both the unborn child and its parents, applying the guideline of love.**

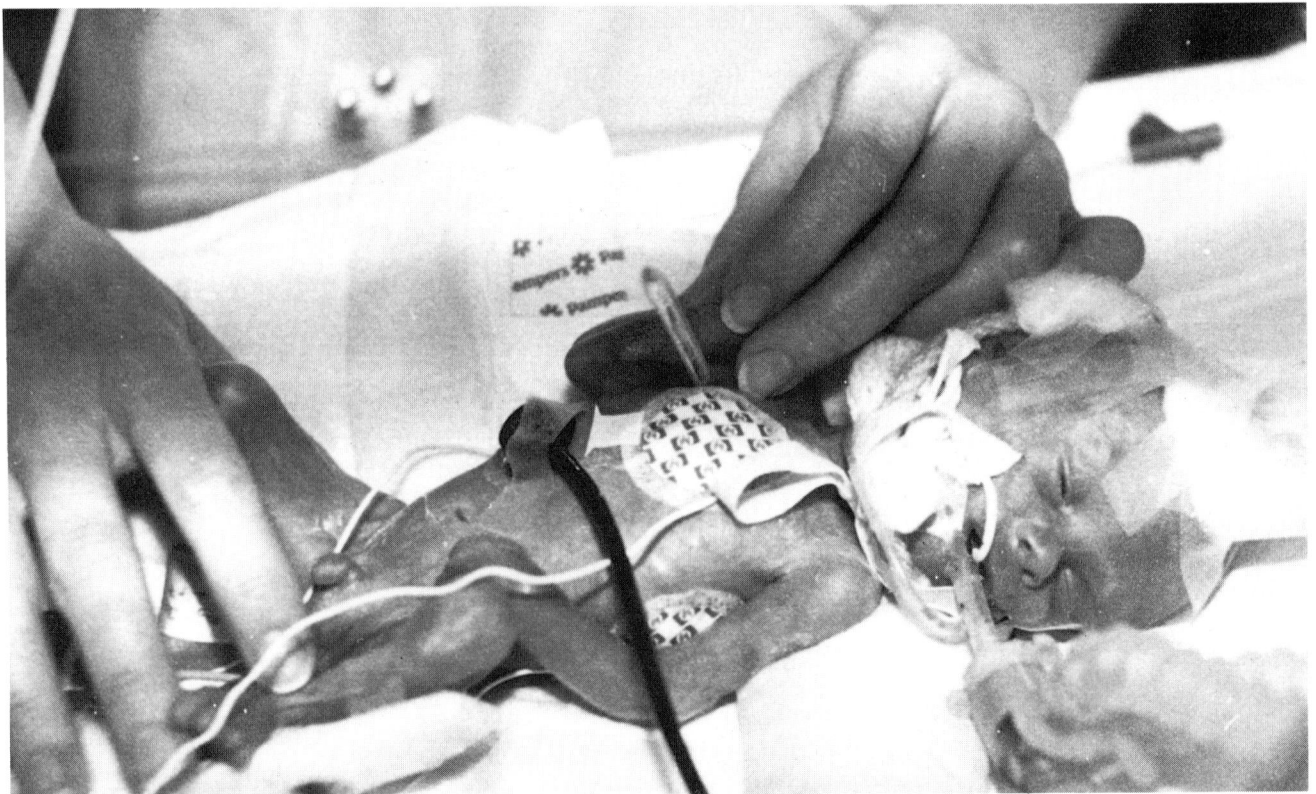

This baby was born during the 23rd week of his mother's pregnancy, and weighed only one pound three ounces. He received special medical and nursing care until, five months later and weighing seven pounds, he was strong enough for his parents to take him home. (Bristol Maternity Hospital; 1984)
   If a woman has an abortion in the 23rd week of pregnancy, the discarded baby might look much the same as this.

CARE OF THE AGED

Christianity follows the Jewish guideline that people should respect and take care of their parents. This is based on the fifth of the Ten Commandments: 'Honour your father and your mother . . .' (Exodus 20:12). Today, when children leave home to marry and set up a family, there are increasing numbers of elderly people who live on their own.

Many Churches make special provision for old people, visiting them, and providing transport to help them attend worship or social gatherings. Some organisations (e.g. the Salvation Army) have special concern for those who are poor and unable to help themselves.

Some old people, if they cannot be with their families, are determined to remain in their own homes. Others welcome the prospect of living with others in a home for the elderly.

- If you were old, which would you prefer – to live with your family, alone at home, or in a residential home for the elderly?

EUTHANASIA

Since 'euthanasia' literally means 'a good death', it is something that everyone hopes for; but the usual meaning of 'euthanasia' is helping a person to die sooner than he or she would do naturally.
Christians generally oppose this for two reasons:

1 The timing of death should be left to God.
2 The final stage of life, once pain and discomfort are controlled properly, can be important, both for the dying person and for his or her family and friends.

The human body is described as a temple of the Holy Spirit (1 Corinthians 3:16), and **all human life should therefore be regarded as sacred.** Catholics oppose euthanasia, along with murder, abortion, suicide and all else that goes against life.

Christians may want to balance these guidelines against the demands of love. For example, a person desperately wounded in battle, with no hope of recovery but the prospect of further pain, may want to die quickly. In such circumstances, a Christian might argue that love requires him or her to help that person to die.

- Do you think it is ever right to help a person to die? Give your reasons and comment on the guidelines given above.

Over to you

1 Look up Ephesians 5:12–6:4. Note down the general guidelines for family life that are suggested by this passage.
2 Look up 1 Peter 3:1–9. Do you think this reflects the relationship between husband and wife in most modern marriages? If not, how might the guidelines given in this passage be applied today?
3 In what way does Jesus' example in John 8:1–11 relate to the guidelines on divorce and adultery given above?

Peace and conflict

INDIVIDUAL VIOLENCE

Jesus taught that his followers should not retaliate when wronged, and they they should pray for their persecutors (Matthew 5:39, 44). When he was arrested, he did not permit his disciples to use force to save him (Matthew 26:51, 52).

Generally speaking, Christians would therefore say that it is wrong to act violently towards another person, but they may seek to justify violence if it is :

- for self-protection, where no other means of defence is available;
- in order to protect or rescue innocent people;
- in order to prevent something happening, the results of which would be far worse than the consequences of the individual act of violence.

An example of the use of the last of these reasons is seen in the German minister and theologian Dietrich Bonhoeffer. He belonged to the 'Confessing Church', a group of Christians which opposed the Nazi party in Germany, and was accused, along with others of an attempt to assassinate Hitler. He was arrested for this, and hanged.

- When, if at all, would you think it right to act violently?

CAPITAL AND CORPORAL PUNISHMENT

Jesus himself suffered both corporal and capital punishment; he was beaten and crucified.

Christians disagree about such punishments. The guidelines they use may include **compassion towards the person convicted of a crime,** and **the need to protect the innocent in society** against people who act violently or commit murder. Following these, some argue that such punishments are right if they deter others. Reform of the criminal is possible through the use of corporal punishment, but not through execution! Retribution ('an eye for an eye'), was opposed by Jesus as a basis for punishment.

Some Christians therefore approve of both capital and corporal punishment, justifying their view by claiming that these punishments may result in a greater good for society as a whole. Article 37 of the *Articles of Religion* of the Church of England states:

> The Laws of the Realm may punish Christian men with death, for heinous and grievous offences.

Other Christians see both capital and corporal punishment as incompatible with the idea of a God of love who creates and values every individual.

Capital punishment is not used in Britain, but in 1989 (according to a report produced by Amnesty International) 2,229 prisoners were executed in 34 countries. (1,500 took place in Iran.)

- Do you think capital punishment is right? In what circumstances? In your answer, relate the general Christian guidelines to the reasons for punishment given above and in the Introduction.

MAJORITY AND MINORITY RIGHTS

Although Jesus' first disciples were Jews, very soon afterwards, the Church contained people of different social and religious backgrounds. St Paul was concerned that these differences should not lead to divisions:

There is neither Jew nor Greek, slave nor freeman, male nor female, for you are all one in Christ Jesus.

(Galatians 3:28)

As Christianity developed into a world-wide faith, it came to include people from a wide range of races and cultures.

The Second Vatican Council, the ruling body of the largest segment of Christianity, meeting in Rome between 1962 and 1965, made the following statement on human rights:

All men have a rational soul and are created in God's image; they share the same nature and origin; redeemed by Christ, they have the same divine vocation and destiny; so it should be more and more recognised that they are essentially equal.

Men are plainly not equal in physical, intellectual and moral powers. But we should overcome and remove every kind of discrimination which affects fundamental rights, whether it be social and cultural discrimination, or based on sex, race, colour, class, language or religion. All such discrimination is opposed to God's purposes.

(*Gaudium et Spes* section 29)

"*In South Africa it is not a matter of Civil Rights, it is a question of fundamental human rights – the recognition that a black person is a human being, created in the image of God.*"

Desmond Tutu is Archbishop of Cape Town and leader of the Anglican Church in Southern Africa.

Examples of Christians campaigning for equal rights for all groups in society may include the work of the South African Council of Churches and the campaign by Desmond Tutu, the Archbishop of Capetown, against racial discrimination in the system of apartheid in South Africa.

Within the Church, Christians are required to set a good example by loving one another. In John's gospel, Jesus is recorded as saying:

"A new command I give you: Love one another. As I have loved you, so you must love one another. By this all men will know that you are my disciples, if you love one another . . ."

(John 13:34, 35)

SACRED AND SECULAR AUTHORITY

Some Christian groups (traditionally called 'pietists') argue that Jesus' kingdom was spiritual and not 'of this world'. They therefore seek to fight only spiritual battles, and may refuse to undertake military service, or vote in elections.

Other Churches (e.g. the Orthodox Churches; the Church of England; the Lutheran Churches in Scandinavia) are more closely associated with secular political authorities. In the case of the Church of England, the ruling Monarch is 'Supreme Governor' of the Church, and the Prime Minister takes part in the process of selecting those who are to be made bishops.

Some take the passage (Luke 20:20–25) about giving Caesar what is due to Caesar, to mean that Jesus' followers should be prepared to obey the political authorities in the country where they live, as well as following the principles of their religion. This is emphasised by St. Paul in Romans 13:

Everyone must submit himself to the governing authorities, for there is no authority except that which God has established. The authorities that exist have been established by God. Consequently, he who rebels against the authority is rebelling against what God has instituted, and those who do so will bring judgment on themselves. For rulers hold no terror for those who do right, but for those who do wrong . . . Therefore, it is necessary to submit to the authorities, not only because of possible punishment but also because of conscience.

This is also why you pay taxes, for the authorities are God's servants, who give their full time to governing. Give everyone what you owe him: If you owe taxes, pay taxes; if revenue, then revenue; if respect, then respect; if honour, then honour.

(Romans 13:1–3a; 5–7)

33

Some Christians refuse to fight for their country because they believe all war is wrong. The Society of Friends (Quakers) have taken this stand and have campaigned for peace.

Some Christian peace protesters are members of Christian CND (Campaign for Nuclear Disarmament).

Read the following extract taken from a newspaper article (*Guardian* 20.4.88) about a Dominican nun, sister Moira, and then answer the following question.

- Why do you think the policeman was confused? Express his dilemma.

'OUTLAW FOR PEACE'

'The first time I was arrested I was wearing my habit and I was moved extremely gently. The policeman was obviously going through terrible agonies about what he should do with a nun . . .'

Her first arrest at Greenham Common in 1983 was for sitting down in front of a truck attempting to enter the air base . . .
She doesn't see nuclear disarmament as an optional extra: 'It's simply involved in the comman-

dment, Thou shalt not kill, as well as the Christian dimension of Love thy neighbour – desperately difficult as this is'.

Not all Christians see nuclear disarmament as the best way to achieve peace, and not all members of the Campaign for Nuclear Disarmament are members of a religion, but for these demonstrators the Christian symbols of peace (the dove) and suffering (the cross) are linked with the symbol for nuclear disarmament.

WARFARE

In the early years of the Church, Christians would not serve in the Roman army and some of its most important teachers – Origen, Tertullian and Cyprian – argued for Christian pacifism. But when Christianity became the official religion of the Roman Empire in the 4th century, all except priests were liable for military service. In 438 C.E. the emperor Theodosius II issued laws inflicting the death penalty on those who did not hold correct Christian beliefs, and insisting that no *non*-Christian could serve in the army!

Some Christians are pacifist and argue that nothing can justify the taking of human life. Others are prepared to go to war, and have developed guidelines to decide when a war is just and how it should be fought.

In the 13th century, the theologian Thomas Aquinas said that three things were necessary for a war to be just:

1 It should not be a private war, but should be waged by the proper authorities in a nation.
2 There should be a good reason for going to war (e.g. in self-defence).
3 The intention should be good (e.g. in order to establish or restore a just peace).

Two other principles may be added to these:

1 Civilians (those who are not military personnel) should be protected during a war.
2 The methods used in warfare should cause no more harm than is necessary in order to achieve the object of the war.

If war cannot be avoided, these rules aim to see that the good achieved outweighs the harm done.

This theory about a 'just war' has led to criticism about the scale of destruction involved in modern warfare. The Roman Catholic document *Gaudium et Spes* (1968) said that:

> Any war aimed at the indiscriminate destruction of cities or wide areas
> [was a]
> crime against God and man,

and *The Church and the Bomb* (the report of a Church of England Commission, published in 1982) argued that:

the cause of right cannot be upheld by fighting a nuclear war.

Christians are divided about nuclear weapons. Some, using the argument about the just war, say that nuclear weapons cause far greater destruction than is necessary in order to win a war, killing civilians, animal life and the whole natural environment. Therefore, such weapons should be eliminated. Others say that it is right to keep them as a deterrent. The threat to use nuclear weapons is so serious that war (even using conventional weapons) may be deterred.

The General Synod of the Church of England, debating nuclear weapons in February 1983, agreed that:

- The government had a duty to guard against nuclear blackmail and deter aggressors.
- NATO (North Atlantic Treaty Organisation, of which Britain is a member) should be defensive.
- All countries should agree not to be the first to use nuclear weapons.
- There should be progressive steps to reduce the number of nuclear weapons.

One might sum up the Christian guidelines on warfare by saying that **some oppose it totally**, arguing that possessing weapons is itself provocative and a threat to peace, that every person is precious in the sight of God, and that true peace and security can only come by solving the world's problems, not by fighting for it. Others say that **war should only be waged with minimum damage to the innocent**, using only sufficient force to secure a return to peace, and should be deterred if at all possible.

- Do you think that it is ever possible for a modern war to be just? In your answer, comment on the guidelines given above.

Over to you

Research information about the Falklands War, both what happened and what views were expressed at the time.

Here are a few brief comments:

In 1982, in response to the landing of Argentine troops on the Falkland Islands, a small British colony, Britain sent a fleet into the South Atlantic, and regained the islands after a campaign in which there was considerable loss of life on both sides.

Argentina claimed that the islands had originally belonged to her and should be returned to her sovereignty.

An argument used in favour of going to war was that the freedom of a British Colony had been violated and that the people of the Falklands had a right to protection, whatever the cost. It was also pointed out that, if the people of the Falklands were ignored by Britain, other small colonies might fear that they too could be invaded.

Those opposed to sending the task force claimed that loss of life could not be justified for the sake of defending islands with a very small population and that the correct way to settle such disputes was by diplomatic means rather than war.

During the fighting, some newspapers in Britain had headlines rejoicing in incidents in which the British troops gained advantage over the Argentinians, in spite of the loss of life that this involved.

The thanksgiving service in St Paul's Cathedral, London, to remember those who had died, included prayers for the Argentine soldiers and their bereaved relatives.

Using this information, and other facts and comments you find about the Falklands War, illustrate the various guidelines that the Christian religion has given for the conduct of war and how they could be applied to that particular situation.

Survivors are helped ashore at Bluff Cove, after the British landing ships, Sir Galahad and Sir Tristram suffer an air attack. (The Falkland Islands; June 1982)

The human qualities of friendship and compassion are important at times like this, but can the suffering of these men be justified by what was achieved?

Humankind and nature

LIFE AND THE ENVIRONMENT

Christians believe that the world was made by God, that it displays a harmony in which everything has a purpose, and that it is good.

The idea of the goodness of creation, found in the Jewish scriptures (the Christian Old Testament), is the main guideline used by Christians for deciding how they should treat the environment.

In the creation story it says:

> God saw all that he had made, and it was very good . . .
> (Genesis 1:31)

This is expressed again in Psalm 148, where all of nature, from the sun and moon to sea creatures, storms and fruit trees are said to praise God.

This idea was taken up by St Francis of Assisi in his *Canticle of the Sun*. He refers to everything around him as 'brother' or 'sister' (e.g. 'brother sun' and 'sister water'), showing that he belongs, with them, as part of a single creation.

In Genesis 1:26–28, humankind is given authority to rule over all other creatures. This suggests that **people should show responsibility towards nature, both to use it for their own benefit and also to take care of it.**

These guidelines, which Christians share with the Jewish faith, are reinforced by two other beliefs:

1 The Incarnation

Christians believe that God took human form on Earth in the person of Jesus, as an expression of his love for humankind and as a means of saving them from sin. This expresses the belief that, since God accepts human form, all human life must be of special value.

2 The Eucharist.

In the central act of Christian worship, found in almost all parts of the Church, bread and wine are taken, blessed and shared. This may be described as

St Francis preaches to the birds: a recognition that all species have their part to play in creation.

a sacrament, in which God is present in a special way and in which people share in the Body and Blood of Christ. The bread and wine, as they are offered in the service, may be described as the fruit of the Earth and the work of human hands – ordinary things, about to be taken up and made holy. This expresses the idea that all of life should be offered to God.

> • If you use or control nature, you may damage it. If you eat something, you destroy it. How do you think a Christian might feel about this, in the light of the guidelines given above?

WORK AND LEISURE

In the Encyclical *Laborem Exercens* (1981) Pope John Paul II said of work:

> Work is a good thing for man – a good thing for his humanity – because through work man *not only transforms nature*, adapting it to his own needs, but he also *achieves fulfilment* as a human being and, indeed, in a sense, becomes 'more a human being'.

Because of this, he argues that the work a person does should not be such as to lower his or her dignity as a human being, in 2 Thessalonians 3:6–10, St. Paul warns against being idle:

> In the name of the Lord Jesus Christ, we command you, brothers, to keep away from every brother who is idle and does not live according to the teaching you received from us. For you yourselves know how you ought to follow our example. We were not idle when we were with you, nor did we eat anyone's food without paying for it. On the contrary, we worked night and day, labouring and toiling so that we would not be a burden to any of you. We did this, not because we do not have the right to such help, but in order to make ourselves a model for you to follow. For even when we were with you, we gave you this rule: "If a man will not work, he shall not eat."

Here it is not so much the work itself that is important, but pulling one's weight within the community.

Work produces wealth. **Christians do not claim that money, in itself, is harmful, but that it is an opportunity for either generosity or selfishness.**

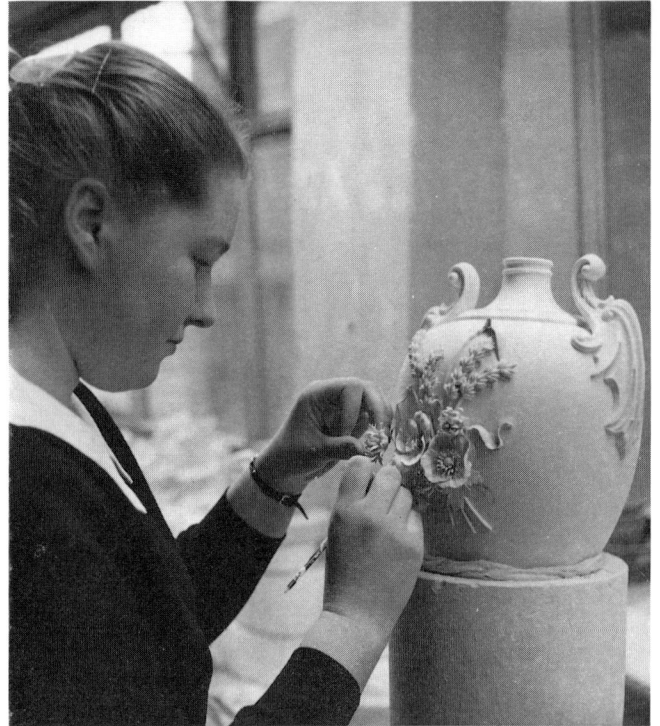

Through creative work, people can fulfil themselves as human beings. What does this very delicate task, finishing off a porcelain table lamp with a poppy and cornflower design, suggest to you about the person who chooses to do such work?

Christians are expected to contribute towards the help of those in need, either directly, through charities, or through their local Church community. Some give a set amount of income, perhaps 10%, for this purpose. In the Middle Ages, the Church would claim a tithe (meaning 'a tenth') of people's produce, in order to support their local priest.

Some choose not to take paid work, either because they wish to concentrate on bringing up children and running a home, or in order to do work on a voluntary basis. There are also monks and nuns who take a vow of poverty, and are supported in their spiritual or practical work by other people.

Some people choose to live in poverty. The argument for doing so is either that it enables them to live alongside and help other poor people, or that they wish to be rid of the hindrance of concerns that wealth brings so that they can concentrate on the life and work they have chosen.

The relationship between work, money and contributing to the welfare of others may not be as simple as the passage from Thessalonians, given above, might suggest.

A warning about money is given in 1 Timothy 6:9, 10

People who want to get rich fall into temptation and a trap and into many foolish and harmful desires that plunge men into ruin and destruction. For the love of money is a root of all kinds of evil. Some people, eager for money, have wandered from the faith and pierced themselves with many griefs.

Christianity does not offer detailed guidelines about how a person should spend his or her leisure time. Some Christians do not approve of any entertainment which involves gambling, but others accept it, provided that it does not become an obsession. Some strict Protestant groups (following the tradition of the Puritans of the 17th century, who banned most forms of entertainment) do not approve of theatres or cinemas, but most Christians feel free to enjoy them if they wish.

Generally speaking, Christianity allows any form of recreation, so long as it does not lead a person to break any of the general Christian moral rules and provided that it does not lead to harm of oneself, other people, or the natural environment.

Sports involving hunting or killing would be opposed by many Christians, because, even if the animal concerned was a pest and its numbers needed to be limited, it would seem wrong to take pleasure out of the act of killing.

Rest should not drift into laziness. Christians, as well as Jews, might want to refer to Proverbs 6:6–11, which contrasts the lazy person with an ant:

Go to the ant, you sluggard;
  consider its ways and be wise!
It has no commander,
  no overseer or ruler,
yet it stores its provisions in summer
  and gathers its food at harvest.

How long will you lie there, you sluggard?
  When will you get up from your sleep?
A little sleep, a little slumber,
  a little folding of the hands to rest –
and poverty will come on you like a bandit
  and scarcity like an armed man.

- Do ants have free will?
  How useful do you think it is to compare humankind with another species? What, if anything, should we learn from the ants?

FOOD, DRINK AND DRUGS

The New Testament does not give precise details about what foods a Christian may eat, but because the Christian community contained both Jews and Gentiles, it was seen as important that all should be able to eat together and that no one person should criticise another over his or her diet. Some who had been used to regulations about food, found their faith tested by this freedom:

One man's faith allows him to eat everything, but another man, whose faith is weak, eats only vegetables. The man who eats everything must not look down on him who does not, and the man who does not eat everything must not condemn the man who does, for God has accepted him.
(Romans 14:2, 3)

- Do you think the author of this passage ate meat?

Some Christians are vegetarians, and some do not drink alcohol, but generally speaking the only guideline is the one in the passage given above – that **a person should be sensitive to the feelings of others. Christians usually agree that drunkenness and gluttony are wrong and that things should be enjoyed in moderation.**

There are no references in the New Testament to smoking or drugs. In deciding about these things, Christians therefore use the general guideline of reason applied to nature and ask what the purpose of these things should be. Some hard drugs (e.g. heroin), used under medical supervision and in small quantities, can relieve pain and improve the quality of life for someone who is seriously ill. On the other hand, if abused, they can lead to misery and death.

Similarly, people who smoke must ask about the harm that it might do to their body and therefore whether they are misusing something which in its natural form is unharmful.

At certain times of the year (particularly in the 40 days leading up to Easter, called Lent) Christians may fast, by going without certain foods or other luxuries. This is not because they are bad in themselves, but so that they can exercise self control and discipline.

- How do you decide what is reasonable and what is a misuse of food, drink or drugs? Which Christian guidelines might help you to decide?

SHARING

Acts 4:32–37 describes the way in which the early Christians sold their private property and distributed it among themselves, so that no-one was in need. This followed the tradition of Jesus' teaching about the Good Samaritan and the Sheep and the Goats, in which **the practical expression of love towards those in need is the most important thing in the sight of God.** James 2:14–17 says:

> What good is it, my brothers, if a man claims to have faith but has no deeds? Can such faith save him? Suppose a brother or sister is without clothes and daily food. If one of you says to him, "Go, I wish you well; keep warm and well fed", but does nothing about his physical needs, what good is it? In the same way, faith by itself, if it is not accompanied by action, is dead.

Living in poverty and hunger: mothers and children wait for aid to arrive at a relief centre during a time of famine. (Mikelle, Ethiopia; 1984). Sharing the Earth's resources with those unable to provide for themselves is seen by Christians as a practical expression of love, and a recognition that everything has been provided by God and should be used responsibly.

Following this guideline, Christians are involved in many agencies, both locally and worldwide, in order to help those in need. Some have been set up by the Churches, others are not organised by members of a particular religion, but are supported by Christians. Among the best known are Christian Aid, Tear Fund, CAFOD (organised by the Roman Catholic Church), Oxfam and Save the Children Fund.

ANIMAL RIGHTS

Christianity does not offer specific rules about the treatment of animals and natural law (the use of reason to understand the natural purpose of everything) traditionally argued that an animal had no 'soul', and therefore had no rights.

Christians keep animals as pets, watch them in zoos, and farm them for meat. In dealing with the most difficult moral choices about animals (e.g. hunting; intensive farming; the use of animals in scientific experiments) there are general guidelines that can be applied:
- Animals are part of God's creation.
- Humankind therefore has authority over them and responsibility towards them.
- If the natural world was created good, then each creature should be allowed to live in a natural way and in an appropriate environment. In other words, you should not force an animal to live unnaturally, preventing it from fulfilling its natural purpose within creation.

- How might you use these guidelines to decide on faming methods?

Over to you

1 Read Mark 10:17–31 and Luke 12:13–21. Use an outline of these two stories to illustrate the Christian guidelines on wealth.
2 How might a Christian argue, using Matthew 25:31–46 and Luke 10:30–37, that there are religious, as well as humanitarian reasons for supporting aid to the Third World.
3 Read Matthew 20:1–16. How might this story be used to justify a 'right to work' campaign?

Islam

Islam is not simply a religion, or a culture, or a set of rules by which to live. A Muslim (one who follows Islam) will probably say that it is the natural way to live, based on worship of God and generosity towards other people.

Muslims believe that the universe is designed so that everything has its particular nature and its own part to play within it. Most things submit naturally and unconsciously to the order and working of the universe, but human beings are an exception: they can either submit to the natural life of the universe, or they can refuse to do so. The word 'Islam' means 'submission'; a Muslim is a person who has submitted to God, the source of life. Every child is born in a state of harmony with nature; therefore every child is born a Muslim. Only later, through the influence of other people, may a child grow up to follow some other religion, or have no religion at all.

'Islam' also means 'peace', and Muslims believe that the natural way of life brings peace, both within a person and between that person and the rest of the world. **The first guideline for a Muslim is that everything should be natural.**

- Other things 'submit' naturally. Why do you think human beings are different from the rest of nature?
- Name a human action or attitude that you would describe as being in harmony with nature and one which might separate a person from it.

ALLAH

Central to Islam is belief in the unity of God (this belief is called *Tauhid*). 'Allah' is not a proper name, but is the Arabic word for 'The God'. Allah is not an idea, nor a person; but is believed to be the source of life of everything in the universe. Islam seeks to bring about a unity and peace with Allah, between people and with the rest of nature. The three worst offences that a Muslim can commit are *kufr*, disbelief (also meaning 'ingratitude' to Allah); *shirk*, associating anything else with Allah – an image, a particular idea, or anything else that might limit Allah; and *tughyan*, which is not to trust Allah, but to act in a way that goes against nature. **For Muslims, everything should promote unity and harmony.**

- Why do you think the idea of *kuft* implies ingratitude as well as disbelief?

QUR'AN AND HADITH

Muslims believe that the Prophet Muhammad, who lived in Arabia in the 7th century C.E., received a revelation from Allah, the exact words of which he recited and which were written down in the Qur'an. Although Muslims accept that there have been other prophets, including Moses and Jesus, they believe that the Qur'an represents God's final and complete revelation of his will for human beings. Muslims therefore accept the Qur'an as the final authority in all questions about life.

Muslims also seek to follow the example of Muhammad (called his '*Sunnah*'). The officially accepted accounts of what he said and did are called *Hadith* (literally 'sayings') and these, along with the Qur'an, provide guidelines for the Muslim way of life.

SHARI'AH

Muslims believe that there is a natural law (called Shari'ah, literally 'path'), established by God, which governs everything from the movement of the planets to the particular behaviour of each creature.

For human beings, their Shari'ah is based on three things:

1 the **Qur'an**
2 the **Sunnah of the Prophet** (as recorded in the Hadith)
3 belief in **the natural unity of everything in Allah.**

Some problems of modern life come from situations which did not exist in Muhammad's day (e.g. things made possible by medical technology). Muslim lawyers therefore apply **'analogy'**. Something may be judged right or wrong, if it can be shown to be the equivalent of something found in the Qur'an or Hadith. The Qur'an says that the Muslim community will never agree together upon an error, therefore Muslim scholars (the *ulama*) sometimes gather to reach an agreement (called *Ijma*) on a point of law. Some Muslims today want the interpretation of the law (called *Ijtihad*) to be extended to involve many Muslims who are not regarded as leaders of traditional scholarship.

If something is lawful for a Muslim, it is called *halal*; if it is forbidden, it is *haram*.

- Can you think of other examples of modern issues, not found in Muhammad's day, for which Muslims might seek guidance?

- Do you think that decisions on matters of law should be left to experts, or taken by a wider number of people? What arguments could be put forward for each point of view?

UMMAH

The Muslim community started in 622 C.E. when Muhammad and his followers left Makkah and made the journey (*Hijra*) to Madinah. Islam dates its years from that event (1990 C.E. is 1410 A.H.). Guidelines for the Muslim life place great stress on the community (called the *Ummah*). Islamic law seeks to protect and create peace and harmony, within the community of Muslims. **A Muslim must be prepared to defend the *Ummah* against** oppression and has a duty to help any fellow Muslim in trouble.

- Some legal systems start with the individual, and show how his or her freedom should be limited to fit in with the needs of others. By contrast, Islam starts with the community, and looks at the part individual people have to play within it.

- Which of these approaches appeals more to you?
- Which seems to be the more natural?
- Which is likely to promote greater harmony between people?
- Discuss your reasons, and suggest examples which illustrate the difference between these two approaches to individuals and the community.

THE DAY OF JUDGEMENT

Muslims believe that all actions, good or bad, are judged by God, from whom nothing can be hidden. People are to be rewarded or punished according to what they have done; and the Qur'an has images of hell as a place of torment and of heaven as being like a beautiful garden.

Because the Shari'ah is the natural form of human life, morality should come from within the individual, rather than being imposed from outside by threats or promises. Yet Islam also insists that a person must be prepared to have every action scrutinised by God and to accept the resulting praise or blame.

By following the Shari'ah, a believer is offered a double benefit – peace in the present and confidence when faced with judgement in the future.

- The Islamic guidelines for life claim to lead to natural peace and fulfilment, but they are also a way of gaining merit rather than blame when judged by God. Which of these do you think is the more important?

- In practice, are you better motivated by thoughts of punishments and rewards, or by inner convictions about what is right for you?

SUMMARY OF MUSLIM GUIDELINES

- *You should do what is natural.*
- *You should promote unity and harmony.*
- *You should support the community of Muslims.*
- *You should obey the law (Shari'ah) as found in the Qur'an and Hadith, and as interpreted by recognised Muslim scholars.*
- *Justice, compassion and generosity are frequently given as qualities of a truly human life.*
- None of you (truly) believes until he wishes for his brother what he wishes for himself.

    (Number 13 from An-Nawai's *Forty Hadith*).

Over to you

1 Here are some things that you should research, they are important for understanding the Muslim way of life:

    (a)   The basic facts about the life of Muhammad; the Hijra from Makkah to Madinah; the early struggles of the Muslim community.

    (b)   The Five Pillars of Islam.

2 The Qur'an lists the rules that Muslims should keep (see Surah 6:151–3 and Surah 17:23–40). Go through these and note down how they illustrate the general guidelines given above.

3 Find out which countries are ruled by Islamic law, and then keep newspaper cuttings and other information about the Muslim lifestyle in those countries.

SHARI'AH AND MODERN SOCIETY

In the following sections, we shall be examining the application of some of the distinctive guidelines for life offered by Islam. In practice, Shari'ah is applied more strictly in some countries (e.g. Saudi Arabia; Iran; Pakistan) than in others (e.g. Tunisia). Although the guidelines remain the same, their application varies from place to place, and may often be influenced by local custom.

Marriage and the family

HUMAN SEXUALITY

Sex, being natural, is accepted by Islam as good, provided that it is enjoyed in the right way. Muhammad declared that, just as a person would deserve punishment from God for unlawful sex, so the right use of sex would bring reward at the Judgement.

It is therefore expected that Muslims will marry and also that they have a right to fulfil themselves sexually. Islam does not teach that there is any religious benefit to be gained from living without sex and so there are no monks or nuns.

Islam seeks what is natural, but also what brings peace between people. Because of this, it insists that marriage is the only context in which sex should be enjoyed. Sex outside marriage is severely punished. Homosexuality is seen as unnatural (and therefore against the Shari'ah for humankind). Adultery causes harm socially (and is therefore against the unity and peace of the Ummah).

- Is it reasonable to say on the one hand that sex is natural and on the other to restrict the ways in which it may be practised? Give your own comments, but also say how you think a Muslim might answer and what guidelines he or she would use.

RULES OF DRESS

When in public, certain parts of the body are to be covered up, so that one person does not tempt

Preparing the evening meal during Ramadan. The girls wear traditional dress, with only hands and face showing.

another sexually. It is a sign of modesty, a recognition that the sexual aspects of the human body are limited to marriage and as a courtesy to the remainder of the community.

For women, the only parts that may be shown in public are the hands and face, while men are required to cover themselves from the navel to the knees. In some countries it is customary for women to wear veils over their faces (e.g. in Saudi Arabia), but many Muslims do not consider this to be necessary and women do not cover their faces while they are on Hajj (pilgrimage). For both men and women the material should be thick enough and loose enough to hide the shape of the body beneath.

These rules only apply to what Muslims should wear in public; in private, husbands and wives are encouraged to make themselves sexually attractive for one another.

- Do you like to dress to attract the opposite sex? What are its advantages? What dangers or misunderstandings might it bring?
- Explain in your own words why a Muslim might choose to wear clothes in public that prevent a person from being sexually attractive.

MARRIAGE

Muslims see marriage as providing the basis for a stable relationship, protecting the partners and any children they may have and offering a suitable means of sexual fulfilment.

The choice of a marriage partner is usually made on the advice of the young person's family and the couple are encouraged to see one another at social gatherings to make sure that their views are compatible, reflecting a similar education and social position. They are not allowed to meet alone and it is assumed that love will develop once they are married, rather than the Western notion that a couple 'fall in love' before they marry.

The basis of the marriage is set down in a contract, which is read out at the wedding, usually by the Registrar (who is called a *Qadi*, literally a 'judge'). A husband is required to provide for his wife, so that she is not required to work or use any of her own money. He also pays over an agreed amount as a dowry (called a *mahr*), which provides the bride with some security and finance of her own. She retains full legal rights over all property she has

before the marriage and retains her maiden name. She can also have the right to divorce her husband written into the contract.

The signing of a wedding contract can be done without any religious formalities, but, since everything has religious significance in Islam, it may take place in a mosque (rather than in the bride's home) and be followed by blessings from the Qur'an and Hadith. Since marriage is seen as a family and a social event, the wedding is celebrated with a party for the families and guests.

A Muslim man may marry a Jewish or Christian woman, provided that any children of the marriage are brought up to be Muslim, but it is not generally acceptable for a Muslim woman to marry a non-Muslim.

- If you could draw up your own marriage contract, what would you include in it?
- Do you think a man should be obliged to support his wife, even if she has her own property or income?

BIRTH CONTROL

Birth control was allowed by Muhammad and is widely practised. Although the sale of contraceptives is banned in Saudi Arabia, other countries (e.g. Egypt and Tunisia) have free family planning clinics.

Some Muslims argue that contraception should be allowed in two situations: where a woman may be harmed by having more children and where a large family may lead to poverty. Others may argue that contraception is wrong because it tampers with the natural laws of life, preventing the normal process of conception. The laws of nature are complex and to interfere with them may cause problems which cannot be predicted.

Muslims fear that, in the West, contraception has been used to avoid the commitment to family life and children for selfish reasons and this they see as going against the Shari'ah for human beings.

Many Muslim couples hope to have a son and will not therefore practise birth control if they have daughters. This is more to do with culture than religion and Muhammad condemned those in his day who allowed baby daughters to die because they wanted the economic benefits that sons could bring.

In Islam, motherhood is seen as a natural and central part of being a woman. Muslims believe that a mother shares in and expresses the creativity of God.

- Explain in your own words how a Muslim might argue for or against contraception, balancing the ideas of compassion and the natural Shari'ah.

POLYGAMY

The Qur'an allows a Muslim man to marry up to four wives, but it sets certain conditions. If a man is to have more than one wife, he must be wealthy enough to provide for them properly. He must also deal equally with them, not favouring one above another. At the time of marriage, a woman may stipulate that her permission is required before her husband is allowed to take another wife and this is

now regarded by some Muslims as a general rule.

In practice, Islam sees monogamy (a single wife) as the ideal and, since it may be practically impossible to deal with absolute fairness with more than one partner, it regards the requirement (in the Qur'an) that wives should be treated equally, as almost the same as a ban on polygamy. For this reason, it has been prohibited in Tunisia, Cyprus and Turkey and is exceptional among Muslims elsewhere. In Syria, Iraq and Malaysia, permission from a court is needed and in Pakistan there is an arbitration council to decide if another marriage is to be allowed.

It may be argued that a husband should take a second wife if the first is infertile, if she is unable to satisfy his sexual needs, if she is ill and needs help with the home, or in time of war when there are a surplus of women who can only be given security within the framework of marriage. The verse in the Qur'an which allows polygamy (Surah 4:3) was revealed to Muhammad after the battle of Uhud while he had the problems of coping with orphans and widows. The argument for having more than one wife is based on compassion for them.

Polygamy should be seen in the context of laws which prohibit adultery. If a man wants or needs another relationship, he must admit it, so that, with the consent of his first wife and while protecting her rights, a second wife may enter the household. Polygamy may therefore provide a stable family situation, where otherwise there would be adultery and divorce. Muslims living in Britain and in other Western countries, are obliged to keep the law of the land and therefore must remain monogamous.

- Imagine a situation where limited polygamy might be an alternative to divorce and monogamy.
  Describe the feelings and problems involved from the standpoint of husband, wife and the other woman.

ADOPTION OF CHILDREN

Muhammad was an orphan, brought up by his uncle; and Muslim children today may be similarly cared for by close relatives. Strictly speaking, adoption is not allowed under Islamic Law. Three reasons are given for this:

1 it is against the natural order;
2 it would deprive other members of the family of

46

their rightful share of any inheritance;

3 in the case of boys, it would give growing young men, who are not blood relatives, access to the women of the family.

Nevertheless, adoption (as well as fostering) is practised, especially where a husband and wife cannot have children of their own. **An adopted child retains the name of his or her natural father, and does not have the right to inherit from the adopting family.** Also, the natural parents always have the right to claim their child back. In some countries (e.g. Morocco) it is quite common for a girl from a poor family to be taken in as 'an adopted maid'. She is not paid for any help she gives in the house, and may call the natural children of the adopting family 'brother' or 'sister', but her natural family may come to visit her several times a year, and she may then return to them later, often when she reaches the age of puberty. This form of adoption is seen by Muslims as an act of charity, and it enables the child to have a good start in life.

DIVORCE

Divorce is allowed, but Muslims believe that to God it is the most hated of all lawful things. When a couple divorce, the man is required to pay his wife any part of the dowry that has been held back at the time of marriage. He must provide for her until she can again be cared for by a man (either by remarriage or from within her family) and provide for any children, who usually remain in the custody of their mother, but may return to their father if she remarries.

A wife can divorce her husband, but must then return the dowry he gave her when they married, unless the marriage breakdown is the fault of the husband, in which case she retains the dowry. In neither case does the man have to provide for her, although he must still provide for the children.

Before divorce is allowed, the couple must have attempted to resolve their differences. If that fails, they must have brought in two friends or relatives to help settle matters. Finally, they must wait for a period of three months (called the *'iddah'*), remaining in the same home, but sleeping separately. This is to see if the wife is pregnant, so that the coming child must be provided for in the divorce settlement and also to see if the couple can come together again.

If either partner ceases to be a Muslim, the marriage is considered to be at an end – a 'mixed marriage' is only allowed at the time of the wedding, not afterwards.

- Note down the ways in which men and women are treated differently in divorce and see how each of these relates to the Muslim attitudes to society and the family.

CARE OF THE ELDERLY

In Islam, families are expected to take care of their older members. Tradition records that Muhammad refused to allow a man to go on Holy War (Jihad) because his father and mother were alive, saying that his first duty was to look after them. **The Qur'an says that you should respect and care for your parents, because they cared for you.**

ABORTION AND EUTHANASIA

Since everything has a natural Shari'ah, a Muslim is reluctant to go against nature. In the case of the elderly or sick person, a Muslim has a duty to show mercy and to care for them. Muhammad prohibited the practice of killing baby girls because they were less profitable to a family than boys. Muslims may use this example to argue against both abortion and euthanasia. Everyone is regarded as a caretaker, with responsibility for the children and elderly in a family.

There is debate among Muslim lawyers about when abortion might be allowed. The Qur'an says that a mother should not be treated unfairly because of her child (Surah 2:233) and this is taken to mean that abortion may take place if the health of the mother is in danger.

Over to you

1 Gather together the information given so far on 'women in Islam'. It may be useful to set out the main themes in a diagram. (You may want to look ahead to the section on 'Work and Leisure' for the position of women at work.)

2 What are the main differences between the life of women under Islamic Law and that in a secular Western society?

3 What problems might a Muslim woman encounter when living in a secular society?

Peace and conflict

INDIVIDUAL VIOLENCE

Since Islam seeks harmony and peace within the community (*Ummah*), it takes the problem of individual violence and hostility very seriously. There is a Muslim tradition that putting things right between people is better than fasting, charity or prayer. The full Shari'ah punishments for murder and theft are severe (see next section).

CAPITAL AND CORPORAL PUNISHMENT

In the Qur'an there are certain fixed penalties, including the death penalty, for serious offences. These are called the *hudud* punishments. Some Muslims regard them as a deterrent to stop crime, others emphasise that they should only be applied once all the circumstances have been carefully examined.

Sensational reports of the death penalty being applied for murder, adultery and homosexuality, or of amputation of the hand for theft, should be seen in context; **they are only used in a minority of cases.** The full Shari'ah, including *hudud* punishments, applies in Saudi Arabia. (The Saudis belong to the Wahhabi sect, a very strict religious group, who interpret the Qur'an rigorously). Pakistan and Iran also apply *hudud* punishments. Other Muslim countries use Shari'ah only for family matters, or for civil actions.

Notice that adultery, fornication or homosexuality, which in a secular society might be seen as a private matter, are treated with great seriousness and may involve the death penalty, whipping or a prison sentence.

In the 19th century, many Muslim countries were ruled by Western nations and were required to use secular codes of law. The return to the Shari'ah is therefore seen as an expression of Muslim identity and freedom from what Muslims may see as the corrupt morality of Western culture.

- Do you think it is right for people to be punished severely for private sexual offences? Using the guidelines in the first part of this chapter on Islam, say how you think a Muslim might argue in favour of this.

MAJORITY AND MINORITY RIGHTS

All Muslims have equal status within Islam, as has every new born child, whatever the religion of its parents. Muslims believe that all authority belongs to Allah and that people are his 'caliphs' (vicegerents), exercising authority only on behalf of Allah. **Everyone is a caliph within his or her own sphere of life, therefore all are equal.** The *Ummah* is not divided on grounds of colour or race. Those who are not Muslims but who live in a Muslim country (called '*dhimmis*') are protected. They have the same rights and responsibilities as Muslims and are allowed to practise their religion. This applies to Christians and Jews (called 'People of the Book'), since they accept the idea of one God and Muslims believe that Moses and Jesus offered people a true revelation. On the other hand, Islam is generally hostile to atheism and secularism and regards those who want to adopt Western or secular views, while retaining the Muslim faith, as a threat to the unity of the *Ummah*.

From the time of Muhammad, Islam united the Arab peoples, leading to spectacular military conquests and expansion. Muslims see this as the result of restoring strength and dignity to each individual – giving power to those who had been submissive. Muslims also seek to restore dignity to non-Muslims who are oppressed.

- In what ways do you think a sense of personal value and dignity can lead to greater strength and achievement?

SACRED AND SECULAR AUTHORITY

Muslims believe that everyting is created and sustained by Allah and obeys (or in the case of humankind, should obey) its Shariʿah. Laws about political and social issues are therefore as much religious as they are secular. Obedience to the law of the land, in a Muslim country, is the same thing as obedience to religious law; there is no conflict. The only problem comes when a Muslim lives in a country that is not run on Islamic lines. In this case, the Muslim is obliged to follow the law of that country, as long as it does not conflict with his or her duties as a Muslim.

Muslims object to secular laws that are not based on the Shariʿah, because they see them as the product of human desires. Secular governments may be voted into power by people who hope to gain something from them. Their laws are not permanent, but may be changed to suit people's wishes. By contrast, governments based on Shariʿah are not seen as depending on human wishes, but as putting into effect perfect justice, since the Shariʿah is believed to have been given by Allah.

- Can you think of any occasions when a Muslim might find his religion in conflict with accepted behaviour in Western countries? (You may find it helpful to look ahead to sections on work, food and alcohol.)
- Can you think of any practical changes that have been made to secular laws (e.g. in Britain) which could not have happened under Shariʿah?

JIHAD

The word 'jihad' means 'striving'; **it is sometimes necessary for a Muslim to engage in a 'holy war' against evil.** There are two kinds of *jihad*: the 'greater' *jihad* is the struggle within the Muslim community and within each person against evil, a form of spiritual discipline; and the 'lesser' *jihad*, which is the struggle against external evils. There are two reasons for declaring a lesser *jihad*:

1 **A Muslim should defend the *Ummah*** (the community of Muslims) if it is threatened from beyond itself. Therefore, if a Muslim country, or a Muslim population of a country, is threatened by non-Muslim invaders or rulers, then it would be right to fight against that threat. It may also be important to fight against those who seek to divide off one part of the *Ummah* from the rest.
2 **A Muslim must be prepared to take up arms wherever there is injustice, on behalf of those who are being oppressed, whether they are Muslims or not.**

The Ayatollah Khomeini, a former leader of the Iranian Muslims, explaining why his followers staged political demonstrations during the *hajj* in 1987, said that it would be impossible to go on

Children growing up in West Beirut are never far from soldiers and weapons. They learn that Muslims should defend those who are oppressed, and fight for justice. But how, in a complex political situation, do you know who is in the right?

pilgrimage and not demonstrate against global oppression. His view was that you cannot have religion without therefore being involved in politics. His views about the pilgrimage were opposed by the Saudis, who see *hajj* as a strictly devotional event and argue for a clear separation between religion and politics. In 1987, 400 people were killed in clashes between the Saudi authorities and Iranian political demonstrators during the *hajj*.

The Muslim responsibility towards one another within the community is extended to include all who are vulnerable. But there are two other rules that apply to *jihad*. **It must only happen as a last resort,** when all peaceful means to protect the community or individual have failed, and **it must be done in such a way as to produce the minimum of suffering.**

In all situations of warfare or punishment, when a Muslim is required to kill or inflict some severe punishment, it must be done with compassion. **It is never part of Islam to inflict pain, only to secure justice.** There is no tradition of 'turning the other cheek' and allowing oppression to continue, for there is an obligation to protect oneself and all other people from injustice.

- During the Russian occupation of Afghanistan, the Mujahadin (Afghan Muslims opposed to the Russian presence) considered themselves to be more than patriots fighting to free their own country. They saw the struggle as a religious duty. Explain in your own words why a Muslim might take that view.

- Do you think it is possible to separate religion and politics? Give your reasons.

Over to you

There are situations in the Middle East where Muslim groups believe that their armed struggle is justified as a *jihad* (e.g. one group in Lebanon calls itself 'Islamic Jihad'). Collect newspaper cuttings and other information on these, and note down any claims they make for a religious basis to their struggle.

Afghan guerrillas with a downed Soviet helicopter gunship, near the Salang highway, north of Kabul.

Were they fighting a jihad, *during the time when the Russian army occupied much of their country?*

Humankind and nature

THE ENVIRONMENT

Central to Islam is the belief that the whole universe is God's creation and that he, Allah, is the source of peace and harmony between humankind and the rest of nature. Islam sees a unity in nature, including all plants and animals, for everything in its natural state is Muslim.

Humankind's role on the Earth is to be a caliph (or *khalifa*), meaning a vicegerent (or trustee) on behalf of Allah. **The Earth does not belong to us; but we are entrusted with its care and we will be held to account (*akhrah*) for how we have acted towards it.**

The general guidelines of natural unity (*tauhid*) and trusteeship (*khalifa*), are turned into practical rules in the Shari'ah. In Muslim countries there are zones which are called *haram* (forbidden), within which development is prohibited in order to conserve natural resources. There are also *hima* areas, which are reserves for wildlife. There are practical laws to safeguard water resources, to prevent over grazing, to conserve forests and to limit the growth of cities.

WORK AND LEISURE

There is a tradition in Islam that it is better for a person to gather bundles of wood to sell, so that Allah might preserve his honour, than to beg from people. **Work is seen as a mark of self-respect,** as well as a practical necessity.

In some Islamic countries it is difficult for women to take paid employment. In Saudi Arabia, for example, women are not allowed to drive cars, or work alongside men. In spite of these rules, a minority of women do manage to run businesses or follow professions.

The public separation of men and women means that, in higher education, some female students receive lectures from male lecturers via closed circuit television. Most women who work outside the home do so in all-women establishments.

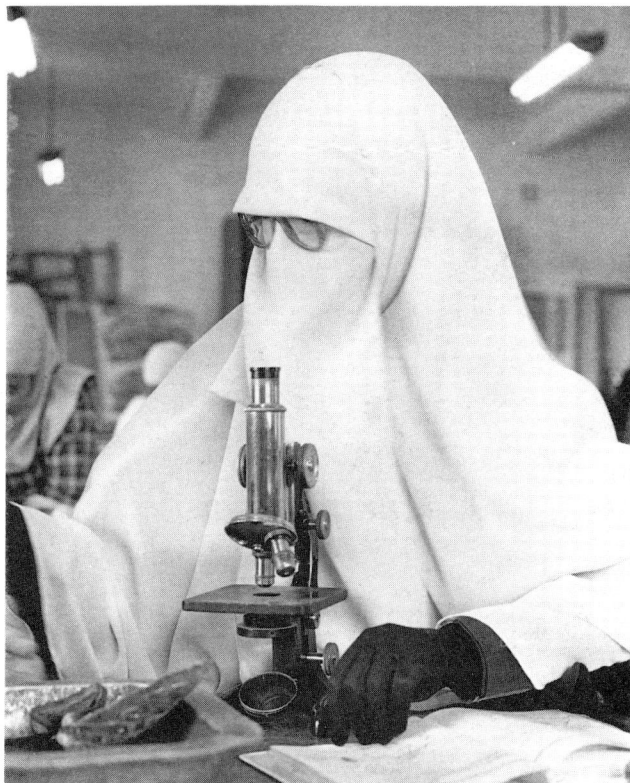

In Egypt, it is now expected that female students with wear the hijab, *a veil covering them completely. Until the 1970's this was rare and is the result of pressure from fundamentalist Muslim groups in that country.*

In Egypt it is now expected that female students will wear the *hijab*, a veil covering them completely. Until the 1970's this was rare and is the result of pressure from fundamentalist Muslim groups in that country.

Muslims see the role of wife and mother as a very important one, so for many women motherhood will be seen as her work, her natural *shari'ah* and her way of acting out her *khalifa*.

In the business community, **Islamic law requires that a just wage should be paid to all employees,** that all deals should be done honestly and that no interest should be taken on loans. Instead of charging interest, Islamic financial institutions may accept a share in the profits of a business venture, which is permitted in Islam.

Because life should be natural and balanced, leisure activities are encouraged. There are four traditionally permitted sports – footracing, wrestling, archery and horseriding.

Leisure activities for women are limited by their exclusion from public events which would involve them mixing with men (*purdah*).

- What is the difference between a business partnership and the relationship between lender and borrower? Why do you think that sharing profits in business is allowed in Islam, but not taking interest on a loan? Try to answer these questions using the general guidelines for life given in Islam.

Saudi princes at the races. In Saudi Arabia men and women do not mix together at public events or work together. This limits the leisure activities open to women.

FOOD AND DRINK

Muslims may eat meat, provided that it is *halal* (permitted). Not all animals can be killed for meat (e.g. Muslims, like Jews, are not allowed to eat pork) and the slaughter must be done in the correct way (see the section on animal rights). Muslims are not allowed any alcohol, and may not sit at a table where alcohol is being served.

Food should never be wasted, and through fasting, Muslims are made aware of what it means to go hungry.

ALCOHOL, DRUGS AND GAMBLING

In the Qur'an (Surah 5:93) alcohol and gambling are condemned because they lead to disputes and hatred between people, and because they stop people remembering God or performing their prayers. Although both may have some value (according to Surah 2:219), the harm they do outweighs this, and they are therefore forbidden (*haram*). This rule applies also for non-Muslims who stay in a Muslim country, although there are generally two exceptions to this: drinking within official embassies and residences and wine used for a religious ritual.

There is a tradition that 'Umar' (a successor of Muhammad, the second Caliph) declared from the pulpit of the Prophet that all drugs which befog the

Muslims praying in a street in Istambul. In Muslim countries, business life may be disrupted at the times for prayer, particularly on a Friday and during the month of Ramadan.

mind are *haram*. As with alcohol, the rule is that if a large amount intoxicates, then even a small drop is forbidden.

Notice that these things are not bad in themselves (both alcohol and drugs may be produced for medical purposes); it is their effects on individuals and the community that leads to the condemnation of their use.

- Make a list of things which are not bad in themselves, but whose use can harm individuals or society.

- Do you think these should be prohibited, or do you think each individual should be left to decide whether to use them or not?

FAMINE RELIEF AND WORLD DEVELOPMENT

He is not a believer who takes his fill while his neighbour starves.

(Hadith: Bukhari p52:112)

All Muslims are required to contribute *Zakah*, money which is given to the poor. In most Muslim countries this is collected by the state, but for Muslims living in Britain, for example, Zakah is collected on a voluntary basis. It is generally set at $2\frac{1}{2}$% of income, and at 10% of the value of jewellery owned. Zakah is not given as a favour, but as an act of worship. Charity is something given over and above Zakah.

Because they are regarded as precious in the sight of Allah, all people have a right to assistance. As trustees of the Earth, Muslims see it as their duty to provide for them, since the money they have is not strictly their own, but has come to them from Allah and is to be used according to his will.

As well as being a most important part of religion (as set out in the Qur'an, Surah 2:172) relief of those in need also brings a reward, for Muslims believe that whoever alleviates a needy person in this life, will be alleviated by Allah, both in this life and in the world to come.

Food should never be hoarded in the hope that its price will rise; and all Muslims are required to fast during Ramadan, as an act of spiritual and physical discipline, reminding them of the facts of hunger and poverty.

In business, the ideal wage paid to a worker is one that allows that person to live at the same standard as his or her employer. This ideal, along with the belief that all people are born Muslim, can be used as a guideline for world development.

Another important guideline for dealing with poverty is the tradition that *jihad* should be waged on behalf of those who are oppressed. Muslims see poverty as the result of the exploitation of people by rulers whose laws are based on selfishness and greed, rather than on the principles of the Shari'ah. By establishing law and justice, Muslims believe that problems of poverty will be overcome.

- What are the main differences between gifts to charity, made in a secular society and Zakah?

ANIMAL RIGHTS

Since the 13th century, Islam has had a legal bill of rights for animals, based on guidelines given in the Shari'ah.

When an animal is to be killed for meat, there are strict rules about how the slaughter is to be done, in order that the animal should suffer as little as possible. It is to be treated with respect and put at ease, before cutting its throat quickly with a sharp knife. While doing this, a Muslim says 'In the name of God, the merciful, the compassionate'. Only animals killed in this way are *halal* and may be eaten.

Respect for animals also means that Muslims do not generally keep pets and do not approve of zoos or circuses. To keep an animal shut in a cage is to violate its natural Shari'ah.

Animals should only be killed for food, never for sport. Muslims believe that, at the judgement a person may be condemned for mistreating or killing an animal for no useful purpose.

The principle of *tauhid*, the Unity of God, links all living things together and requires that Muslims show respect towards every creature.

Over to you

Turn back to the summary of Muslim guidelines on p. 43. Then make notes on how these have been applied to the various issues raised in this section. Make sure you understand why Islam responds as it does to each of these issues.

I S L A M

53

Hinduism

Hinduism is not a single religion, but is the name given to a whole family of religious traditions and a way of life that has developed in the Indian sub-continent. People from these traditions do not generally call themselves 'Hindu', but may say that they are devoted to Krishna, Shiva, or one or more of the many gods and goddesses, some worshipped throughout India, others known in only a single local shrine.

Because of this, it is impossible to lay down guidelines that apply to all Hindus. What is more, unlike Judaism, Christianity or Islam, Hinduism does not depend for its guidelines on detailed interpretation of sacred scriptures. Although some sacred writings (e.g. the Gita or the Ramayana) are popular and form the basis of many images and festivals, they are not used in order to explain or argue for a particular action, as might happen with a verse from the Bible or the Qur'an. Some devout Hindus follow their traditions of worship without ever reading sacred scriptures, learning and handing on their traditions orally.

In spite of the great variety, there are certain guidelines which apply to Hinduism as a whole and it is these, rather than details of particular traditions, that we shall be looking at in this section.

DHARMA

Dharma means 'right conduct' or 'duty'. For an individual Hindu, his or her *dharma* sets out the guidelines for life. It depends mainly on two things – who you are, and what stage you have reached in your life.

WHO YOU ARE

In Hindu society, people are divided into four main caste groups (called *varnas*). Within each *varna* there are many sub-divisions, called *jati*, usually based on the particular work that people do. When Hindus speak of 'castes' they often refer to these sub-divisions, rather than to the four *varnas*. A person cannot change his or her caste, but is born into it, although in cities people of different castes mix far more than they do in villages.

Brahmin
This is the priestly caste, and is generally the most highly educated. Brahmins traditionally work in education and in spiritual guidance. Of the four castes, only the Brahmins are traditionally allowed to teach from the Vedas (the Hindu scriptures).

Kshatriya
This is traditionally a 'warrior' caste. Kshatriyas hold military and administrative posts and are concerned with the maintenance of law.

Vaishya
These are the 'merchant' caste. They include business people and those skilled in agriculture. (Today there is some flexibility between these three castes, with Kshatriyas, for example, holding university posts.)

Shudra
This is the lowest of the varnas. Shudras are generally manual workers.

The caste system does not say that one caste is better than another, for society needs all of them to work together, but it asserts that different people are born with different abilities, and that it is better for them to recognise and follow the life for which they are best suited.

YOUR STAGE IN LIFE

There are four stages in life (called the *ashramas*), each of which has different duties, and requires particular personal qualities.

1 Student
At this stage a person should work hard, show respect and obedience to teachers and parents, and live a disciplined life, abstaining from sex, alcohol, smoking and drugs.

2 Householder
From the age of 25 a person should take responsibility for home and family life and follow a career. Of the four stages in life, the rules for this one are the most lenient, because of the practical demands and commitments of everyday life.

3 Retired
From the age of 50 and traditionally with the arrival of a grandchild, husband and wife may start to distribute their goods to their family and to retire from active life. Together, they should detach themselves from household and family concerns.

4 Ascetic
Sometimes, from the age of 75, men may become wandering 'holy men' living very strictly, with few possessions and no luxuries (which is what the term 'ascetic' means) in order to be devoted to religion. Such a man is called a *sadu* or a *sannyasin* (although this last term is also used for younger followers of some Hindu sects).

These four *ashramas* do not apply to Shudras, nor to women. Few men go through all four stages. **The 'householder' state tends to last from teenage years often through to the end of life.** Few are prepared to give up their worldly concerns at the age of 50. Therefore, in considering Hindu guidelines, it is the second *ashrama* that dominates society.

- The Hindu guidelines for life may sometimes be referred to as *varnashramadharma*. Break this word down into its three parts, and use them to write an explanation of what it means.

- Does *varnashramadharma* apply to non-religious people in a secular society? Think of examples of behaviour that are appropriate or not depending on age or social position.

- At what age do you think a person is ready to run a household and at what age should you retire?

THE GOALS OF LIFE

Hindus should follow their *dharma* and in doing so may hope to achieve three other things:

1 kama
This means 'pleasure', including sexual happiness and a general enjoyment of life.

2 artha
This is 'wealth', general prosperity and the satisfaction of ordinary physical needs.

3 moksha
This means 'release'. Hindus believe that all creatures take part in a process called *samsara*, in which, at the end of life, each is reborn as another creature. The next life (whether as a plant, an animal, a low caste human or a brahmin) depends upon actions, good or bad, that are performed in this life. These actions are referred to as good or bad *karma*.

Following one's *dharma* correctly not only brings present happiness, but also builds up a store of good *karma*, which can cause a person to have a better rebirth in the future.

Samsara (rebirth) is not seen as a blessing, but as a constant struggle from which a person would choose to be released. **Moksha (release) is therefore the most important goal for a Hindu.** It represents a spiritual perfection in which the individual is completely united with God.

Through the stages of life, a Hindu will therefore try to cultivate a detachment from worldly concerns.

Although Hindus use many different religious images, they are believed to be expressions of a single, universal reality, called *Brahman*. Release is achieved when your inner self (your *atman*) is at one with the universal *Brahman*.

- Does the idea of an endless succession of lives (*samsara*) appeal to you? Give your reasons.

PERSONAL QUALITIES

As well as the guidelines laid down by your particular caste and state of life, there are personal qualities which are recognised by all Hindus as leading to good *karma*. Some of these are:

- generosity
- self-control
- purity
- insight
- wisdom
- compassion
- friendliness
- forgiveness
- cleanliness
- avoiding anger
- not stealing
- fortitude
- patience

Each person should cultivate these and avoid their opposites, within his or her particular *dharma*.

Although it is difficult to generalise about Hindu moral teachings, the five principles observed by the followers of Satya Sai Baba, would be accepted by many Hindus as basic to their way of life. They are:

- *Satya* (truth)
- *Dharma* (right conduct)
- *Shanti* (peace)
- *Prema* (love)
- *Ahimsa* (non-violence)

Individuals find that they have different abilities and different personalities. A quality which comes naturally to one person is difficult for another. Hindus believe that we have different personalities because of *karma* accumulated in previous lives.

- Are you responsible for your own personality, or are some things beyond your control?
- Some qualities suit members of a particular caste. Which caste would most benefit from: Mental discipline? Physical stamina? Skill with weapons? Insight? Bravery? Business skills?

SUMMARY OF HINDU GUIDELINES

- *Follow the **dharma** appropriate to your caste and stage in life.*
- *You may enjoy pleasure and wealth, but be aware that the final goal of life is **moksha** (release).*
- *Develop your positive qualities, especially trying to show compassion (non-violence) towards all other living things.*

Over to you

1 Read chapter 2 of the Bhagavad Gita, a most popular Hindu scripture. Note down references in it to the guidelines given in this section.
2 Look up the names and characteristics of some of the main gods in Hinduism – particularly Brahma, Vishnu and Shiva.
3 Find out about the sixteen steps that a Hindu will take through life and the ceremonies that are associated with each of them.

Marriage and the family

SEX

Human sexuality is not regarded as a spiritual hindrance in Hinduism, but is welcomed as a positive and natural part of life and as a valid source of pleasure.

When they reach the appropriate age, Hindus are expected to marry and have a family. Those in the 'student' stage in life, being unmarried, are to abstain from sex, as are those who reach retiring age. Traditionally, at the age of 50, a couple who

Erotic sculpture on the remains of a Hindu temple.

retire together should cease to have a sexual relationship, but live together as companions. Few Hindus today choose to enter this third stage of life.

Many religious images depict sexual activity. The god Krishna is sometimes shown as a cowherd, playing a flute. His music is said to make the cowgirls fall in love with him and he is sometimes shown dancing with his favourite, called Radha. There is also a story about Krishna stealing the cowgirls' clothes while they were bathing, so that each had to come out of the water naked in order to retrieve them. These stories are meant to symbolise God's love for each individual; and nakedness shows that nothing can be hidden from that love.

Kama (pleasure) is one of the aims of life, and the *Kama sutra* is a religious text which encourages physical sex to be enjoyed in a way that makes it become a religious experience.

The god Shiva is often represented by the *lingam*, the upright penis, as a symbol of fertility.

Hinduism emphasises the positive value of human sexuality, and by depicting ideal relationships (e.g. between Krishna and Radha, or between Rama and Sita, in the Ramayana) it offers an image of religious devotion and examples for people to follow.

- Some religious groups have regarded sex as either nothing to do with religion, or else as harmful. Hinduism sees it as having positive value as an expression of love and creativity. How might these views affect your attitude to relationships and to your own body?

The god Krishna is shown here with Radha. His love for her expresses his love for all his worshippers and also gives an example of a perfect relationship which couples may want to imitate.

MARRIAGE

Traditionally, marriage partners are chosen for young people by their families and marriages are arranged only between those of the same caste and jati.

This remains the situation in many places, but among Hindus living in Britain, young people will often make up their own minds about whom they wish to marry, although parents may arrange introductions to likely partners. In the West, young Hindus of the opposite sex may meet at school and socially in a way that would not be possible in India.

Hindu religious tradition states that a girl should be at least 14 years old and boys 18, before marriage, but girls have to be older where this is required by the law of the land (16 years in Britain).

At one time, young children were married and then stayed with their own parents until puberty (at which point the girl moved in with her husband's family). This is no longer permitted.

- Hindu parents might argue that romantic love between young people is an illusion, based on sexual attraction and that choice of a marriage partner requires a matching of temperaments, educational and social backgrounds. Do you agree with this?

- Indian newspapers often carry advertisements placed by those looking for marriage partners. What would you want to say about yourself in such an advertisement? What would you look for in a likely marriage partner?

Three sets of rules apply to marriage:

1 The Law of the Land
In India, this accepts any form of religious ceremony as a valid marriage. In Britain, marriage must be registered, and this is generally done at a Registry Office before the Hindu wedding.

2 Customary Law
This varies from one place to another, as do all Hindu religious ceremonies.

3 Brahmanical Law
These are the rules that apply within almost all Hindu traditions, and are based on scriptures (the Vedas).

Until 1961, it was expected that a girl's family would provide her with a dowry when she married – cash or goods which were handed over to the bridegroom and his family at the wedding. This is now officially banned in India, although it is customary for the girl to offer gifts. Dowries were (and gifts may still be) a matter of dispute and negotiation between families, with the bride (who lives within the groom's family after the marriage) sometimes being victimised for not having provided what was expected.

- Do you think that it is right for any gifts to be negotiated between families as part of a marriage agreement? Why do you think the practice has continued, even if unofficial?

There are many variations of the wedding

ceremony. Priests devise their own, based on rules given in the Vedas (Hindu scriptures) and local customs. Certain features are common, and the following represent particular Hindu guidelines on marriage:

- The bridegroom may ask the bride to touch or stand on a stone. This represents stability; she and their future family, are to be stable like a stone.
- Rice grains may be thrown into the sacred fire. These represent fertility, and express the hope that the couple will have children.
- The couple usually walk seven times round the *arti* flame (a sacred fire), or they may step on beetle nuts seven times. The seven things represented by this are: food; good health; wealth; good character; children; happiness; friendship. During the last circuit, the couple have their clothes tied together. They hold hands and promise to be united in mind and heart.

The seven steps before the sacred fire (not necessarily around it) were set down in the *Manusmrti* (a handbook of *dharma* by Manu) as the one necessary feature of a marriage, which is therefore considered to have taken place once the couple have finished the seventh step.

- The bridegroom may place a traditional wedding necklace round the bride's neck. This has black beads, and two semicircles of gold, one representing the bride's family and one the bridegroom's. This is a reminder that the wedding unites two families, as well as the two individuals.

Hindus believe that the creator god Brahma is within everything and unites everything. Therefore loving your marriage partner is a part of loving yourself. It is also believed that fulfilling one's duty as a husband or wife produces good *karma*.

In the **Ramayana** epic, Rama, who is an *avatar* (incarnation) of the god Vishnu, wins the hand in marriage of Princess Sita. When he is banished from the kingdom that he rightly should be ruling, Sita volunteers to go with him and faces many dangers as a consequence of her loyalty. When she is captured by the demon Ravana and taken off to Sri Lanka, Rama rescues her and the couple return to rule in their kingdom.

This story, celebrated in two important Hindu festivals (Dashera and Diwali) is taken to express the victory of good over evil, but it also represents the ideal of marriage, with faithfulness to one another triumphing over suffering.

PARENTHOOD AND FAMILY LIFE

Once married, it is expected that the wife will take charge of all the household arrangements and finance. Her husband will not be expected to take any share in the housework.

- Do you think it is better if one partner takes complete control of domestic life, or is it better shared equally? Which would you prefer if you were about to be married?

Hinduism is a religion centred on the home and family. The following comment on family life comes from Manu, whose laws form the basis of much Hindu practice:

Where the women are respected, there lives God. If the wife is obedient to the husband, and the husband loves his wife; if the children obey the parents, and guests are entertained; if the family duty is performed and gifts are given to the needy, then there is Heaven, and nowhere else.

In traditional Hindu society, people live in extended families, as sons marry and introduce their wives and then children into the home. Cousins living together may sometimes refer to one another as 'brother' or 'sister', which may be confusing for those who do not know the family.

Four generations of a Hindu family meet together – great grandmother, grandparents, parents and children. What are the advantages and disadvantages of living together as an extended family?

Having a large number of children was traditionally thought of as a mark of prestige, especially if there were sons. Daughters were less popular, since they could not continue a family business, but were destined to marry and help in their husband's home. A Hindu man cannot hope to escape from *samsara* (rebirth), nor have any rewards in paradise before being reborn, nor even enter into the last stages of life, until he has produced a son! For this reason, although contraception is practised among Hindus, there are social pressures against it.

Members of the Krishna Consciousness movement oppose contraception on the grounds that sex is permitted in order to conceive Krishna Conscious children – in other words, sex should continue to have its natural creative function.

ADULTERY AND DIVORCE

Although divorce is not actually forbidden in Hinduism, it is frowned upon, and many would not consider applying for a divorce if they follow Hindu guidelines strictly.

Divorce is possible if a husband is cruel, or if a couple have been unable to have children after fifteen years of married life. Adultery on the part of the husband is not considered, in itself, to be an adequate ground for divorce, for the Law and Manu states that a woman should respect and obey her husband, even if he is unfaithful. Remarriage after divorce is legally possible, but rare.

- Do you agree that a woman should continue to respect an adulterous husband? Give your own views, but also comment from the standpoint of the Hindu guidelines.

CARE OF THE AGED

There is an expression in Hinduism that your father is an image of the Lord of Creation, and your mother is an image of the Earth. **Honouring them is therefore a person's first duty; and if you fail to do so, then all other religious ceremonies are useless.**

Because of this, as in all cultures where there are extended families, care for elderly people tends to take place within the family home.

Following the traditional four stages in life, some people might choose to retire and be on their own,

or even, in the case of a man, become a wandering *sadu*, but this is unusual.

Many Hindus today feel that caring for elderly parents is a task that is just as valuable spiritually as becoming a *sadu* and retiring from life.

ABORTION AND EUTHANASIA

Following the guideline of *ahimsa* (non-violence), Hindus oppose all taking of life – including abortion and euthanasia.

Gandhi, whose whole life and work was to promote non-violence, said that *ahimsa* might permit killing if it were founded on a totally unselfish motive, in order to bring about some spiritual benefit. Indeed, this might be the 'purest form of *ahimsa*'. Each case of killing, therefore, would have to be judged on its own merit. There is a possibility that some cases of euthanasia could therefore be compatible with the idea of *ahimsa*.

- Do you think euthanasia is compatible with the Hindu guideline of *ahimsa*? Give your reasons. It may be helpful to look at the section on Individual Violence in 'Peace and Conflict'.

Over to you

Hindu guidelines for marriage and family life were established in a culture which was based on the extended family. Hindus in Britain today are increasingly tempted (or forced by economic circumstances) to follow their neighbours in society, and live in nuclear families (parents and children, separate from other relatives). Some may delay having children and women may take work outside the home.

Find out all you can about Hindus living in Britain (or another Western country) and then go through the issues covered in this section, noting the cultural and religious problems that might arise as a result of these social changes.

Peace and conflict

INDIVIDUAL VIOLENCE

There are two traditions within Hindu thought – the ascetic and the social.

The ascetic tradition
(i.e. the tradition based on the denial of physical comforts for the sake of spiritual benefit) is best illustrated in the life and work of **Mahatma Gandhi**. He argued that *ahimsa* (non-violence) should be the main guideline for life. Its opposite, *himsa*, is used to describe both killing and causing pain or injury. Although it is usually the result of anger or selfishness, Gandhi recognised that all life, since we must eat, requires the destruction of something outside ourselves. **No living thing can be completely non-violent. Nevertheless, as a goal *ahimsa* requires that a person should live thoughtfully, in a way that requires him or her to inflict the absolute minimum of suffering on other creatures.**

Gandhi said that, if you were guarding someone and were attacked, you should place yourself between the attacker and the person in your charge. You should receive whatever wounds the attacker inflicted, without offering any retaliation, so that all his or her anger was expended on you alone.

This principle was used in Gandhi's non-violent campaign against the British rule in India.

- Following the ascetic tradition, what practical consequences would follow from trying to achieve the absolute minimum of violence?

The social tradition
In Hindu thought this is based on the second stage of life – that of the householder. It too approves of the principle of non-violence, but, in order that society may be organised and ruled for the benefit of everyone, it allows violence to be used in certain circumstances. The question is, how should a good person act towards a violent one? The answer to this, in the social tradition, is quite different from that of Gandhi.

In *Manusmrti* (the law book of Manu), it says that a person is not guilty if he or she kills an assassin. **Killing is therefore possible on two conditions:**
- **to prevent something worse happening;**
- **if it is necessary, to maintain social order.**

The concept of *ahimsa* in the Vedas does not extend to include non-violence towards enemies in war, criminals, wicked people and offending animals. It is also permitted to kill an animal for the purposes of one's own livelihood.

Mahatma Gandhi took non-violence as his principle guideline. Is it possible for a human being to be totally non-violent? Would you retaliate if attacked?

Within both the ascetic and social traditions there is the further idea that *himsa* (violence) should not be limited to physical harm, but should include such things as restricting the speech, thought or freedom of another person.

- Following the 'social' guidelines, suggest some practical situations in which you think it would be right for a Hindu to use violence.
- Whose views on the use of violence do you prefer – those of Gandhi or those of Manu? Explain why.

CAPITAL PUNISHMENT

Following the social tradition, guidelines for capital punishment are set down in the *Varaha-Purana*. A king may put a criminal to death and a person who is considered to be evil may be executed by any available means. This restores justice and the correct *dharma* in society.

A lesser criminal may be helped to return to his right *dharma* by being reformed through punishment and through teaching him or her how to live properly.

Since killing in self-defence is permitted under the laws of Manu, capital punishment may be seen as self-defence on the part of society as a whole, where a criminal cannot be reformed.

- How would you set about deciding if a criminal is beyond being reformed?

MINORITY RIGHTS

As well as the divisions between castes and jatis, India itself consists of twenty-three states, its people speak fourteen major languages and between 300 and 400 local dialects. The whole of India may therefore be seen as a collection of minorities. The Tamil people of South India, for example, see themselves as descendants of the Dravidian people, who occupied India before the invasion of the lighter skinned Aryan peoples who settled in the north of India in about 1500 B.C.E.

The Dravidian people are thought to have been non-violent, agricultural people, very different from the warlike Aryan tribes. Some scholars explain features of modern Hinduism in terms of the mixing of these two very different traditions. Something of this is suggested in the section above on 'violence'. (About seventy per cent of British Hindus come from the state of Gujarat in the north-west of India, and therefore do not necessarily represent the whole variety of Hindu life.)

Hinduism speaks of minorities in terms of *dharma*. Each group in society, like each individual, has its part to play within the life of the whole. Each of the castes depends upon the others for its life. Even the lowest people in the social scale have their role, by performing the tasks that those of higher castes would not wish to do. **The guideline for dealing with minorities is therefore interdependence.**

Gandhi was concerned about those who were at the very bottom of the caste system and were known as **'untouchables'**. In the early years of the twentieth century, they were not allowed to enter public buildings, nor to attend government schools. They could not use public wells for their water supply and could only travel by train in a special compartment reserved for them. He called them **'Harijans'**, which means 'Children of God' and tried to see that they had their basic human rights.

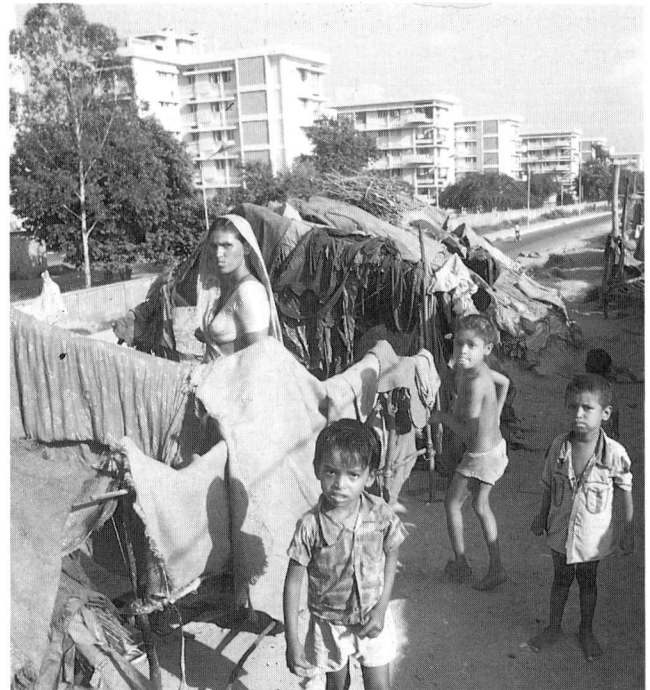

Harijans living out in the street in Delhi, across the road from modern flats.

In 1950 the Indian Constitution outlawed untouchability, but it is a difficult law to enforce as local custom still determines what happens in most areas. 'Harijans' generally prefer to be called *Ardi Dravida*, 'original Dravidians'. They tend to perform the most menial of work and to live, often in extreme poverty, on the edge of society.

Untouchability is a problem within Hinduism, and many religious people are concerned about these divisions within society.

> • In India there are 'untouchable' Christians, Buddhists and Muslims, as well as Hindus. Do you think it is possible for a religion to go against the long-held traditions of a society?

Although they are not a 'minority', women have traditionally accepted a role rather different from that of men in Hindu society.

Hindus would not say that women are in any way inferior to men, but that their physical and psychological features make it natural for them to accept the guidance and protection of men.

In the past, with child marriage, and the suicide of some widows (*sati*) on the funeral pyre of their husbands, women lived by a *dharma* which would not be acceptable today. Although traditionally involved with home and family, an increasing number of Hindu women (especially those who have moved to the West) now have work and interests outside the home.

SACRED AND SECULAR AUTHORITY

Because there is such variety, it is difficult to generalise about how Hindus deal with secular authority. Here are two well-known examples:

Mahatma Gandhi (1869–1948)
He wanted India to achieve independence from the British. He insisted on non-violence, but led a campaign of civil disobedience and protested in such a way that he exerted pressure on the government. In order to improve the conditions under which people were living, he worked to change the secular law by spiritual means.

Vinoba Bhave (1895–1982)
He was a follower of Gandhi who wanted land to be redistributed from the wealthiest to the poorest, as a means of overcoming poverty. He did not oppose the secular law, which allowed ownership of land, but worked to persuade people to give away some of their land voluntarily. Starting in 1948, in the first six years his *Bhoodan* movement had organised the redistribution of four million acres of land. He worked to solve this problem by trying to change the attitudes of individual people, rather than altering the secular law.

Rulers have their *dharma*, just like everyone else and they have an obligation to organise society. Hindus respect this, but (as the above examples show) may also want to change the way in which society works.

WARFARE

The *Bhagavad Gita* is part of the *Mahabharata*, a long poem describing the rivalry between two families, the Kurus and the Pandavas. In the *Gita*, Arjuna, a prince of the Pandava family, finds his conscience troubled by the idea of going into battle to kill the opposing Kurus because the two families are related. The *Gita* describes a conversation between Arjuna and his charioteer, who turns out to be the god Krishna.

Krishna tells him that he must fight, because it is his *dharma* to do so. He also points out that the true self (or soul) cannot be killed.

> If any man thinks he slays, and if another thinks he is slain, neither knows the truth. The Eternal in man cannot kill: the Eternal in man cannot die.

Later Krishna says

> Think thou also of thy duty and do not waver. There is no greater good for a warrior than to fight in righteous war. There is a war that opens the doors of heaven, Arjuna! Happy the warriors whose fate is to fight such war.

> Prepare for war with peace in thy soul. Be in peace in pleasure and pain, in gain and in loss, in victory or in the loss of a battle. In this peace there is no sin.

The *Gita* expresses the conflict between the 'ascetic' and the 'social' guidelines. On the one hand there is the principle of *ahimsa* (Arjuna does not want to take life), but on the other is the idea of

Troops of the Indian Army on parade. Although they may accept the ideal of non-violence, Hindus sometimes believe that they have a duty to fight.

They should do so in order to secure justice and without using excessive force.

dharma, which requires some people to be involved in warfare. The two pieces of advice given would seem to be:
- **do your duty, but detach yourself from the results, being content whatever the outcome;**
- **deeper understanding of the nature of life and death will remove the problem.**

> - Which do you think should come first – duty or conscience?

The *Manusmrti* gives rules for the right conduct of a war. You should not kill any of the following: a person who surrenders; anyone who joins his hands in a gesture of supplications (in other words, a person who can no longer threaten you, and who asks for mercy); anyone you come across while he is asleep; a person who is disarmed; an onlooker, not involved in the battle; an enemy who is wounded; women and children.

Manu also sets limits to the sort of weapons that should be used. Arrows should not be barbed, poisoned, or blazing.

In other words, even if the social tradition of Hinduism does not accept a pacifist guideline, warfare should be controlled and should respect the individuals involved in it, not causing unnecessary suffering.

> - How might the laws of Manu be applied to modern warfare? What sort of weapons would not be allowed today?

Over to you

Look at the advice on warfare given above from the *Bhagavad Gita*, and if possible, read the *Gita* itself. Notice two important principles: (i) the true soul is not killed by physical death; (ii) good *karma* is the result of doing your *dharma* and for a soldier this may involve killing.

Now imagine a dialogue between two people about to go into battle and, like Arjuna, feeling troubled in conscience about it. Let one of them be a Hindu and the other a person with no particular religious allegiance.

Either act out a dialogue between them or write down how you think each would justify to the other his or her participation in the coming battle.

Humankind and nature

LIFE AND THE ENVIRONMENT

There is a Hindu saying:

The Earth is our mother, and we are all her children.

Hindus believe that everything in the universe, both living things and inanimate matter, is an expression of God. In the *Gita* (6:27–31) Krishna speaks of the Yogi (the person who follows spiritual discipline):

Thus joy supreme comes to the Yogi whose heart is still, whose passions are peace, who is pure from sin, who is one with Brahman, with God.

He sees himself in the heart of all beings and he sees all beings in his heart. This is the vision of the Yogi of harmony, a vision which is of oneness.

He who in this oneness of love, loves me in whatever he sees, wherever this man may live, in truth this man lives in me.

Thus the ultimate spiritual goal for a Hindu is to see and love God in and through everything. Nature is not something to be exploited, but something to be identified with and loved.

Many Hindu gods (each of which is an expression of the one Brahman) appear as animals (e.g. Hanuman is a monkey; Ganesh is elephant-headed), thus reminding the worshipper of qualities to be found in the animal world. The god Vishnu is believed to have had many *avatars* (incarnations), one of which is as Krishna. In earlier ones he takes the form of various animals, each of which manages to save the world from a particular danger.

Alongside these animal images in worship, there is the whole idea of *samsara* (rebirth). Although it is a caricature of Hindu belief to say that you are reborn as an animal if you behave like one in this present life, there is an element of truth in it. All creatures are bound up together in the great wheel of *samsara*.

The essential idea for Hindus is that people do not own the world around them, they belong to it and love God in and through it.

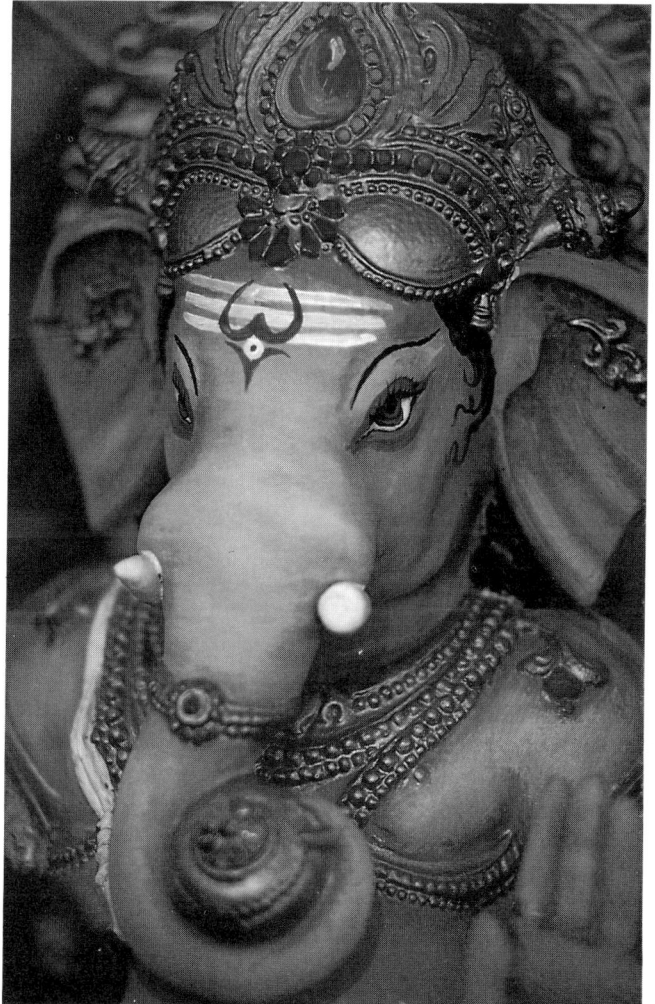

Elephants are intelligent, hard working and good at removing obstacles. Hindus may pray to the elephant-headed Ganesha when they need these qualities.

65

- Try to express the vision of the Yogi, given in the passage quoted above, in your own words.

- How, in practical terms, might this vision affect a person's treatment of the environment?

Ahimsa (non-violence) is another important guideline for Hindus in dealing with life and the environment. They will try not to harm any living thing. This is particularly important in the treatment of animals (see later section).

WORK AND LEISURE

In traditional Indian society, the work that a person does is determined by his or her caste (see the opening section on Hinduism). Often an Indian village will be physically divided up into little areas, where people from particular *jati* (sub-castes) carry out their craft or trade. In these circumstances, the work a person does is usually determined by the family and community and particular skills may be passed down from one generation to the next.

Among middle-class, professional Hindu families in Britain, academic success and good professional qualifications are seen as important goals for their young people to aim at.

Most Hindu women are expected to work within the home, caring for children and fulfilling all their other domestic duties. In some situations, however, that traditional role is changing. Here are three examples:

(i) In Madras, the Stree Seva Mandir was set up by Mrs Krishna Rao in order to train and provide work for women, many of whom were destitute and had children to support. The women support themselves by producing goods for sale and also train in various crafts. This aims to allow them to become independent and self supporting.

(ii) In Britain, a number of young Hindu girls, as they come to the end of their time at school, choose to follow a career, rather than to become married straight away. Sometimes their parents accept this, but it may cause friction between the generations.

(iii) Among some Asian communities in Britain, up to eighty per cent of women now take paid work in order to contribute to the family finances. In the extended family situation, children are often looked after by a mother-in-law or other relative, living either in the same house, or nearby. The size of an average family is decreasing among Asian Hindus, and more are now living as nuclear families – all of which changes the sort of work that women are expected to do.

- Do you think it is right for traditional Hindu parents to persuade a girl to marry, rather than follow a career?

- What dangers might lie in putting career before marriage?

Looking at the way some people live in Western society, Hindus might comment that the balance between work and leisure is being spoiled by anxiety. People may work in order to get money, in order to enjoy themselves and yet, however much they get, they remain dissatisfied.

A Krishna Consciousness booklet advises:

> Everything in the material word is influenced by time. Nothing which we can construct, no effort which we can make and no wealth we can amass, will last for ever. It is because of the influence of time that everyone is anxious.
>
> When we see ourselves and others as eternal parts and parcels of Krishna, and when we are satisfied by our service of Him, then there is no need of anxiety and enviousness.
> (from *An Introduction to Krishna Consciousness*)

From a Hindu perspective, it is only through spiritual satisfaction that people can enjoy both work and leisure.

- If leisure and wealth do not last, are they worth all the effort of working for them?

- Which is better, to work because it is your *dharma*, or to work in order to gain wealth? Can you aim for both at once?

FOOD AND DRINK

Following the guideline of *ahimsa* (non-violence), most Hindus are vegetarian. Those who do eat meat are likely to refuse beef, since the cow is held in special respect. In India, there are regional variations in diet; for example, Bengalis, who live in the north, will often eat fish, which would be refused by those who come from the southern states.

In the West, Hindus may give a variety of reasons for having a vegetarian diet. A follower (devotee) of Krishna Consciousness may argue that:

– A devotee will only eat food that has first been offered to Krishna; but in the *Gita*, Krishna says that he should be offered fruit and vegetables.
– Meat eating is unhealthy, since meat may contain preservatives and poisons and because the human digestive system is developed to cope with vegetable foodstuffs.
– Humans can live quite well without slaughtering innocent animals.
– We may suffer for it, because, if we needlessly kill animals, 'we will have to be slaughtered and eaten in our next lives.'

Krishna Consciousness devotees abstain from meat, fish and eggs and also from intoxicants: alcohol; tobacco; drugs; tea and coffee.

Within Hindu society there are many other food laws, generally related to caste. Brahmins will usually only eat rice if it has been cooked by another Brahmin, but will accept vegetables cooked by anyone. Lower caste Hindus may sometimes drink alcohol, but Brahmins do not.

Hindus sometimes fast – going without food, or having a restricted diet, for a fixed period of time. This is generally done in honour of one of the gods; it is thought to bring religious merit and also to improve self-control and physical well-being.

SHARING

A Hindu may carry out five daily obligations: to worship God; to pay respect to holy men; to honour his or her parents; to give shelter to guests; to feed animals.

The last two of these give practical expression to the general guidelines of generosity and compassion, which were listed among the personal qualities that a Hindu should try to cultivate.

To follow the fourth of the obligations, a Hindu may actually receive guests into the home, or may give something as charity for the benefit of the poor. Hindus also have a tradition of generosity towards members of their extended families and those from their village community.

- What advantages might there be in having *daily* obligations to be carried out for either religion or society?

ANIMAL RIGHTS

The last of the five daily duties of a householder is to make offerings to all creatures and this may take the form of placing food on the ground outside the home at the four cardinal points.

The practical result of this is that it can be shared with wild and stray animals and it provides a constant reminder that humankind shares life with many other species.

All creatures are related to one another through the process of *samsara* (rebirth). Hindus therefore try to respect and preserve all forms of life. The *Yajurveda* (13:47) says:

No person should kill animals helpful to all. Rather, by serving them, one should attain happiness.

The cow is particularly respected by Hindus, as a symbol of the kindly and harmless quality of life. Here a cow wanders freely in the street in India. It may hold up the traffic: is that a nuisance, or an important reminder of Hindu values in the world of business and city life?

Over to you

1 To appreciate how Hindus think and feel about the environment, it is useful to reflect on the idea of God being within the self and within everything. Suggested reading for this: *The Bhagavad Gita*, especially chapter 13; The *Kena Upanishad* part 1; *The Chandogya Upanishad* section 6:12 (this contains the famous statement about the self and God being at one, as well as the analogies of dissecting small seeds and salt in water).
2 Since Hinduism is rooted in the life and culture of India, try to gather information about life in the sub-continent today, perhaps from newspapers, and relate it to the guidelines given in this chapter.

Buddhism

Buddhism offers a practical set of guidelines for life, following the teachings of Gautama Buddha, who lived in northern India in about the 6th century B.C.E.

It is not based on belief in God or gods, but is a system of training, exploring the principles by which life operates in order to lead people to insight and a natural harmony, both within themselves and with the world in which they live. **A Buddhist might say that his or her aim is to overcome the sufferings caused by greed, anger and illusion while moving towards a state of peace, joy and enlightenment, which is called** *nirvana.*

Buddhists believe that all actions (*karma*) have their consequences. What you do or think today will affect who you are tomorrow, so that foolishness will keep a person trapped in a world of craving and rebirth (*samsara*). There are no external threats in Buddhism, nor are there absolute, fixed rules. **The qualities of gentleness, compassion and serenity, which a Buddhist will try to develop, should come from inner conviction and personal responsibility, not as a result of guilt or fear of punishment.**

> • What do you understand by the word 'religion'? Should Buddhism be called a religion if it is not based on belief in God?
>
> What we are today comes from our thoughts of yesterday, and our present thoughts build our life of tomorrow: our life is the creation of our mind.
>
> (Dhammapada 1)
>
> • In what ways might your thoughts and decisions affect the future?
>
> • Which is better, to have moral rules given to you from outside, or to develop them for yourself? Give examples to illustrate your answer.

THE FOUR NOBLE TRUTHS

The starting point for the Buddhist guidelines for life is expressed in four statements:

1 All life involves suffering (*dukkha*). This is not just physical suffering, but the sense that life is unsatisfactory, never quite what we hoped for.
2 The cause of suffering is craving (*tanha*). *Tanha* means trying to cling on to what changes, wanting to control everything.
3 When craving ceases (*niroda*), so does suffering. A person can then find inner peace.
4 The way to stop suffering is to follow the Middle Way (*magga*).

Five things hinder a person's progress:
● greed
● hatred
● laziness
● restlessness and worry
● doubt, indecision and lack of trust
These show the kind of life from which Buddhism seeks to release people.

> . . . whoever in this world overcomes selfish cravings, his sorrows fall away from him, like drops of water from a lotus flower.
>
> (Dhammapada 336)
>
> • Can you think of any practical situations which might illustrate this?

THE MIDDLE WAY

This describes a way of life that is neither ascetic (rejecting all comforts in the hope of spiritual benefit) nor luxurious; its guideline is moderation.

It is set out as a path of eight steps (The Noble Eight-fold Path) which leads a person towards enlightenment – the state of being fully awake to the truth of life, like Gautama Buddha.

Of the eight steps, five deal with the right thoughts and intention that a person should have and the mental training (meditation) that is needed in order to follow this path. The remaining three steps offer these guidelines:

Right speech
Buddhists should avoid lying, telling slanderous tales, speaking harshly or chattering aimlessly. All speech should be helpful and show others respect.

Right action
This is summed up in the *Pansil*, the five principles which all Buddhists try to observe. The positive reason for each is given in brackets.
- I will not take life (to show compassion to all creatures).
- I will not take what is not given (to be generous and honest).
- I will not misuse sex (to let sex be natural, causing no harm, but expressing contentment and love).
- I will not lie (to be truthful in all I say).
- I will not use drugs or alcohol (to keep my mind clear and alert).

Right livelihood
You should work in a way which does not go against the five precepts, or principles.

The Middle Way outlines the teaching (called *Dharma*) which applies to all Buddhists. Monks and nuns (the *Sangha*) have their own special rules and disciplines, set out in a book called *Vinaya Pitaka*.

THE FOUR SUBLIME STATES

In meditation, Buddhists may think about four qualities (called the Four Sublime States, or *Brahma Vihara*). Thare are: **love** (towards all creatures, as well as oneself); **pity** (compassion for all who suffer); **joy** (an unselfish sharing of other people's happiness); **serenity** (freeing oneself from anxiety about success or failure). These four qualities form personal guidelines for Buddhist thinking and living.

CHANGING ATTITUDES

Buddhists would claim that their spiritual training not only brings personal benefit, but influences their relationships and attitudes to other people. Each person can therefore contribute to the improvement of everything. Buddhists therefore tend to solve problems by changing attitudes, rather than by simply obeying rules or devising technical answers.

> There are those who argue that we shall be able to overcome all our global difficulties through technological advance – an outward-directed solution. I prefer to believe that the true and necessary revolution is spiritual and inward-directed. Until people can re-evaluate civilisation from a less selfish and materialistic viewpoint, they will find it hard to identify the sources of renewal and enrichment which can form the basis of a better, more positive future for the human race as a whole.
>
> Daisaku Ikeda

- Daisaku Ikeda, a Japanese Buddhist, here argues that the answer to human problems lies in new attitudes, rather than technology.

  Do you agree with him? Give examples to illustrate your answer.
- From the guidelines already outlined, suggest what changes in attitude a Buddhist might seek.

SUMMARY OF BUDDHIST GUIDELINES

- *Work to develop a sense of inner peace and satisfaction, so that you can enjoy life.*
- *Cultivate love and compassion towards all other creatures.*
- *Always act thoughtfully, aware of the consequences of what you do.*
- *Be prepared to adapt your guidelines to meet the needs of each situation (i.e. 'using skilful means').*

Over to you

1 Read an account of the life of the Buddha and note how it illustrates The Middle Way.
2 Look up the following in a textbook on Buddhism: **The three main branches of Buddhism; ideas of 'the self' and 'rebirth'; the six paramitas; the ideal of the Bodhisattva; the Three Universal Truths (*anicca, dukkha, anatta*).** These will provide useful background information for your understanding of the guidelines.

Marriage and the family

SEXUALITY

One of the five basic precepts for all Buddhists is to refrain from the misuse of sex. This means that, although sex itself is regarded as natural and good, it should not be practised in a way which may hurt people.

Many modern Buddhists say that both heterosexual and homosexual relationships can be of value, but traditional Buddhists may not approve of homosexuality. What matters is that sex should be an expression of love and trust and should not be used in an attempt to solve emotional or other problems.

Lust is regarded as one of the hindrances to spiritual growth. It is therefore important for Buddhists to use and enjoy sex, but not to be controlled by it. Married Buddhists are expected to be faithful to one another.

There is a strong tradition of monastic life (the *Sangha*) in Buddhism, especially in Theravada and Tibetan Buddhism. In the Theravada tradition, lay Buddhists are anxious to support the *Sangha* and regard the monks and nuns as nearer to achieving Nirvana. The monk (or nun) does not give up sex because it is a bad thing, but because the distractions of sexual partnerships and family life are thought to hinder those engaged in spiritual and mental discipline. In the monastic life, a person is freed from all such distractions and responsibilities.

On the other hand, the *Mangala Sutta*, which devout Buddhists may recite each day, lists among those things which are an 'auspicious performance' (in other words, things which bring about a blessing):

Supporting one's father and mother, cherishing wife and children, and a peaceful occupation; that is the most auspicious performance.

So family life itself is respected in Buddhism.

Most Buddhists marry and share in family life, but some choose to join Sangha, *the community of monks and nuns. This monk lives in a monastery in Hertfordshire, his shaved head and robes are expressions of his commitment to following the spiritual path.*

- How important is it to be free from distractions if you want to develop spiritually? Should sexual and family relationships be seen as an obstacle or an opportunity for personal growth?

MARRIAGE

Marriage itself is not a religious event in Buddhist countries, but after having their marriage registered, Buddhists may wish to receive a blessing from monks in a Vihara.

This blessing may include these traditional promises made by the bride and bridegroom. They are taken from the *Sigalovada Sutta*, which may be two thousand five hundred years old. They may not all apply to modern Buddhist marriage.
The bridegroom says:

Towards my wife I undertake to –
love and respect her,
be kind and considerate,
be faithful,
delegate domestic management,
provide gifts to please her.

The bride says:

Towards my husband I undertake to –
perform my household duties efficiently,
be hospitable to my in-laws and friends of my husband,
be faithful,
protect and invest our earnings,
discharge my responsibilities lovingly and conscientiously.

- Do you think it is right for the wife to undertake all the domestic and financial responsibilities?

- Would you prefer husband and wife to make identical promises to one another, or do you think the Buddhist ones are more realistic?

In Western countries, the marriage ceremony usually takes place during a regular Buddhist gathering, with promises like these made by bride and groom.

In some countries there are other ceremonies used at the wedding. For example, in Thailand the couple kneel side by side, while each guest pours a little holy water over their hands. This and other customs are accepted within that culture, but are not a necessary part of the Buddhist religion.

The same thing applies to the choice of marriage partners. In some communities, marriages are often arranged between the families of bride and groom, but in others (for example, among people in Britain who have been converted to Buddhism) it is more likely to be a personal decision made by the couple.

PARENTHOOD

Buddhism teaches that parents have a responsibility to provide for their children, to teach them the Buddhist guidelines for life, to see that they have a proper education, and to help them to become established in a suitable marriage.

In Buddhist countries, orphaned children may be adopted and cared for by uncles and aunts, or by other members of their extended family. Buddhists would see this as a natural expression of compassion and love, two of their most important guidelines.

Buddhists are equally concerned to show compassion towards those orphans who cannot be cared for by their extended families, and some organisations (e.g. the Tibetan Young Buddhist Association) state that one of their aims is to construct and run orphanages.

INHERITANCE

In most Buddhist countries, it is usual for the inherited wealth from parents to be shared equally between their children. The eldest child has responsibility to organise and see that this is done fairly.

DIVORCE AND ADULTERY

The Buddhist ideal is that a married couple should remain faithful to one another. Factors which lead to divorce, like intolerance, resentment, hatred, restlessness or lack of trust, are all regarded as hindrances to spiritual growth. The Buddhist guidelines are therefore aimed at freeing a person from those things which lead to unhappiness in marriage.

The Buddha taught that, once a man married, he should look on all women other than his wife as though they were his mother, his sister or his daughter, so that even the thought of committing adultery could be considered as harmful.

Four things happen to the thoughtless man who takes another man's wife: he lowers himself, his pleasure is restless, he is blamed by others, he goes to hell.

(Dhammapada 309)

Buddhists would not describe adultery as a sin to be punished, but as an action by which a person can bring upon himself or herself certain harmful consequences. This self-inflicted punishment is what is meant by 'going to hell'.

- An absolute rule that must not be broken, or a guideline (with warnings about self-inflicted harm) – which is more realistic (or more useful) in considering sexual faithfulness?

CARE OF THE AGED

There is a tradition that the Buddha was asked 'Who are the gods?' to which he answered 'Let father and mother be your gods.'

This expresses the importance that Buddhism places on compassion within the family. A married couple should be prepared to support both their parents and their children and also, where necessary, to help others within their families. It is therefore usual for the elderly to be cared for within the family home.

For those not cared for in this way, Buddhists support residential homes for the elderly, as another expression of the guideline of compassion.

ABORTION AND EUTHANASIA

Buddhist teaching states that new life begins as soon as sperm and ovum meet. This means that all abortion is killing and therefore harmful karmic effects.

A Buddhist may decide (for example, in the case of a child likely to be born with a severe handicap) that, having considered the alternatives, it is right to have an abortion. In this case, those involved recognise that it may result in a certain amount of personal suffering, because every action (*karma*) has its personal consequences.

The same guidelines could be applied to euthanasia for a person who is seriously ill. The Buddhist Hospice Project, an organisation set up in Britain to help those who are dying, sees the process of dying 'as an opportunity for spiritual growth both for the person dying and for the carers'.

Practical care and support are therefore offered as a positive alternative to euthanasia.

Over to you

The guidelines of 'love' (*metta*) and 'compassion' (*karuna*) are the basis of Buddhist teaching on marriage and the family.

Go through each of the issues outlined in this section and list the ways in which these two guidelines are applied to it.

Peace and conflict

INDIVIDUAL VIOLENCE

The first of the five precepts (*Pansil*) to be observed by all Buddhists is that they should not take life. **Violence and murder harm not only the victim, but also the person who acts violently, for it destroys inner peace.**

'He insulted me, he hurt me, he defeated me, he robbed me.' Those who think such thoughts will not be free from hate.

For hate is not conquered by hate: hate is conquered by love. This is a law eternal.

Many do not know that we are here in this world to live in harmony. Those who know this do not fight against each other.

All beings tremble before danger, all fear death. When a man considers this, he does not kill or cause to kill.

(Dhammapada 3, 5, 6, 129)

- Imagine that you are about to act violently towards someone. What thoughts or feelings might you experience? In what way might they destroy your inner peace?

CAPITAL PUNISHMENT

Buddhists generally oppose capital punishment for two reasons. Firstly, it involves the taking of life and this is against the first of the Pansil – the five basic precepts for the Buddhist way of life. Secondly, Buddhists believe you should show compassion towards those who have done wrong – trying to reform them if possible. In spite of this, the laws in some traditionally Buddhist countries allow capital punishment for serious crimes, like murder or dealing in drugs.

POLITICAL ACTION AND HUMAN RIGHTS

Buddhists sometimes protest against the secular authority under which they live. They may justify this by saying that 'Right Government' is the result of applying the principle of 'Right Livelihood' to the life of a country as a whole.

In Japan, Soka Gakkai, a modern organisation which follows Mahayana Buddhist teaching, campaigns for peace and claims that the only way humankind is going to escape destruction is by setting itself against violence of any sort. Because of this, Soka Gakkai was suppressed by the Japanese government during the Second World War, but was re-established in 1946.

In 1988, Buddhist monks were prominent in demonstrations against the government in Burma, but they also acted as mediators between the military and the demonstrators in order to seek an end to violence.

Similarly, in 1987 and 1988 there were demonstrations in Lhasa, the capital of Tibet, against the Chinese rule there. The lamas (Tibetan Buddhist religious leaders) and other monks were involved for both political and religious reasons, wanting independence and more freedom to promote Tibetan Buddhism. Although the Chinese originally closed many of the monasteries, Buddhism remains important for Tibetans and is now increasing there.

Some Buddhists choose to suffer in order to protest against injustice or violence.

I am young and I don't want to die. But I have seen the sadness of my country and if my death can help, it will be worthwhile.

I have immense faith in Buddha and in His Holiness (the Dalai Lama). I believe that if I die I will be reborn to a better future in the next life.

These comments were made by Gedun Shakya, aged 22, one of a dozen Tibetan exiles who were preparing to start a hunger strike to protest at the Chinese occupation of Tibet.

Similarly, during the Vietnam War, some Buddhist monks burned themselves to death in public as a protest against the violence.

In contrast to this, other Buddhists think that any suicide is wrong. It is a crime equal to theft, since it does violence against the body, which shares in, and expresses, the Law of Dharma and should be treated with compassion like any other creature.

- What is your own view of those who go on hunger-strike in order to promote their cause? What do you think they achieve by their action?

WARFARE

A man is not a great man because he is a warrior and kills other men; but because he hurts not any living being he is in truth called a great man.

(Dhammapada 270)

Following the first precept (not to take life), Buddhists oppose warfare. In Britain, the Buddhist Peace Fellowship helps Buddhists to organise themselves for demonstrations in favour of peace.

In extreme circumstances, some Buddhists may be tempted to take a different point of view. In 1988, The Dalai Lama (the spiritual leader of Tibetan Buddhists, who fled into exile in India in 1959) ceased to demand full independence for Tibet and suggested that it might have self-government, although with China still maintaining troops in the country. This was opposed by Lhasang Tsering, president of the Tibetan Youth Congress, who said

We consider violence against the Chinese as self-defence.

and

There have been no cases of Tibetan hijacks or kidnappings.

Others have obtained a platform by these means, but no government supports us.

Although contrary to Buddhist guidelines, this expresses the frustration of living in a world where violence is assumed to be a means of achieving political results.

- Which is more important, to stick by your principles, or to achieve your goal, even if it means going against those principles? What dangers lie in either choice?

The Peace Pagoda at Milton Keynes. The beauty and simplicity of its design expresses the Buddhist hope that all people will live together in peace.

Over to you

1 Explain as fully as possible, using the Buddhist guidelines, the action of the monks as described in the newspaper extract on the next page.
2 From your understanding of the Buddhist guidelines, outline the dilemma faced by a Buddhist contemplating a hunger strike.

Buddhist monks join people's fight

Terry McCarthy reports from Rangoon:

'One of the most unforgettable aspects of the uprising in Burma has been the sight of Buddhist monks in the thick of the demonstrations, mediating, directing and safeguarding people, and at the same time calling for democracy.

Despite the Buddhist aversion to confrontation and violence the monks, or *pongyis*, in Burma have a long tradition of political involvement, particularly in times of anarchy or oppression.'

'. . . Before the military takeover, when the whole country was on strike, the monks organised after-dark security in Rangoon. They took government infiltrators, suspected of poisoning water, into their custody to save them from beheading. They also organised the distribution of rice in poor areas when food became scarce . . . (They) took possession of the weapons of army deserters. Angry crowds of students wanted to keep the guns . . . monasteries became safe havens for students and other activists.'

Humankind and nature

REVERENCE FOR LIFE

Life itself is the most precious of all treasures. Even the treasure of the entire universe cannot equal the value of a single human life.

Daisaku Ikeda

All Buddhists hold human life to be of great value. Mahayana Buddhists may express this through the idea that every person has a 'Buddha nature', the potential to develop the same qualities as the Buddha and to achieve enlightenment. Buddhists should also seek the welfare of all living beings.

THE ENVIRONMENT

As the bee takes the essence of a flower and flies away without destroying its beauty and perfume, so let the sage wander in this life.

(Dhammapada 49)

Buddhists see the whole universe as a single vast living thing; humankind does not stand over against nature, but is part of it. Everything depends upon everything else. The forces of cosmic life that produce a human being simultaneously bring about the environment in which he or she will live – and the one is not possible without the other. Care of the environment is therefore a central attitude for Buddhists. The Japanese term for this is *esho funi* (the unity, *funi*, of living things, *esho*, with their environment, *eho*). If all forms of animal and plant life depend on one another for their common existence, then care for other creatures will also enhance human life.

As a practical expression of this, businesses run on Buddhist principles would try to waste the minimum of fuel and packaging material and re-cycle whenever possible.

- Is it possible to live without hurting your environment in some way? What practical steps could you take to limit any damage?

WORK AND LEISURE

If a man when he is young and strong does not arise and strive when he should arise and strive, and thus sinks into laziness and lack of determination, he will never find the path of wisdom.

(Dhammapada 280)

Guidelines on leisure are provided in the Sijalovada Sutta, where the Buddha warns a young man against six things which can lead him into poverty – drinking; love of theatre and feasts; evil companions; gambling; idleness; and wandering about the town at night!

Idleness and a harmful use of leisure time are therefore criticised because they can lead to poverty and because they show that a person is living in a thoughtless way. Money is not seen as good in itself (and a Theravadin monk will avoid handling money), but for lay Buddhists (i.e. those that are not monks or nuns), work is necessary in order to provide for members of their family and in order to have the means to show practical compassion to others and support good causes. Even a monk is required to provide food for his parents, if there is no one else to take care of them.

In business dealings, Buddhists are required to be honest. Employers should treat their employees fairly and with an understanding of their abilities and their needs.

In Britain and other Western countries, the Friends of the Western Buddhist Order have set up businesses in order to support members of their community and pay for the Buddhist activities they organise. Following the principle of 'right livelihood', their work is chosen to be compatible with Buddhist principles (e.g. a vegetarian restaurant; a wholefood shop; a bookshop).

Following the second of the precepts (do not take what is not given), Buddhists should never work in a way that exploits other people.

- What problems might a Buddhist businessman encounter in a Western capitalist society?

FOOD AND DRINK

Many Buddhists are vegetarian, since they do not want to kill animals for food; but no foods are actually forbidden, so it is a matter of personal choice. Monks will generally eat meat if it is offered to them, since it would be wrong to refuse a gift, but they may reflect with sorrow on the death of the animal as they eat it.

Some Buddhists argue that a vegetarian diet makes the mind clearer for meditation and makes a person healthier, but most Tibetan monks eat meat, as do those whose physical work means that they get particularly hungry and may not feel satisfied with a vegetarian diet.

Most Buddhists do not use alcohol, tobacco or other drugs which tend to cloud the mind. The whole basis of Buddhism is awareness of life and this would be hindered by intoxicants. Other Buddhists argue that a little alcohol does no harm.

- Clouding the mind is not limited to drink and drugs. What else in our society might be described as 'mind numbing'?

Mind numbing?

HELPING THE POOR

Misers certainly do not go to the heaven of the gods, and fools do not praise liberality; but noble men find joy in generosity, and this gives them joy in higher worlds.

(Dhammapada 177)

Compassion (*karuna*) is one of the qualities (the *Brahma Vihara*) on which Buddhists meditate. Offering gifts (*dana*), especially food to the monks, is a feature of Buddhist life that aims to cultivate an attitude of unselfishness. Buddhists in wealthier countries may organise aid for those in the Third World. The Friends of the Western Buddhist Order, for example, operate the Karuna Trust, which supports hostels and health education projects in slum areas in India.

A nun receives offerings of food at a monastery in Sussex. By offering gifts (dana) and especially by giving food to monks and nuns, Buddhists try to cultivate an attitude of unselfishness.

ANIMAL RIGHTS

Buddhism teaches non-violence and compassion towards both human and non-human life. In the 1986 Assisi Declarations on 'Man and Nature', in which each of the major religions contributed a statement about its attitude to the environment, the Abbot of Gyuto Tantric University said:

> The simple underlying reason why beings other than humans need to be taken into account is that, like human beings, they too are sensitive to happiness and suffering: they too, just like the human species, primarily seek happiness and shun suffering. The fact that they may be incapable of communicating their feelings is no more an indication of apathy or insensibility to suffering or happiness than in the case of a person whose faculty of speech is impaired. . . . We should . . . be wary of justifying the right of any species to survive solely on the basis of its usefulness to human beings.

Buddhists therefore oppose the hunting of animals for sport, breeding them for meat in unnatural conditions, or misusing them in any way. Animals are to be respected in their own right.

- Do you have a pet animal? If so, does it communicate its feelings to you? How might this influence the way you treat it?

Over to you

1 Make a list of occupations which (following the five precepts of 'Right Action'), a Buddhist would not want to follow.
2 From the information given in this section and referring back to the general introduction to Buddhist guidelines, describe in your own words how each of the following Buddhist ideas may influence a person's relationship to the world in which he or she lives:
   a) the universal 'buddha-nature';
   b) compassion (karuna);
   c) the unity between each thing and its environment (*esho funi*).

Sikhism

Guru Nanak (1469–1538) was the first of ten *gurus* (or teachers) whose followers are known as Sikhs (a word which means 'follower' or 'disciple'). Sikhs believe in one God and base their lives on the teachings of the ten Gurus and on the Sikh holy book, the Guru Granth Sahib.

Sikhs believe that, without the inspiration that comes from devotion to God, people live in a state of illusion (*maya*), in which their attitudes are dominated by five evil impulses (lust; anger; greed; attachment to worldly things; pride). **A Sikh hopes for release (*mukti*) from illusion and the cycle of birth and death, into the presence of God.**

Sikhism is a way of life that emphasises practical goodness. The qualities that a Sikh should develop are:

- self-control
- forgiveness
- contentment
- love of God
- humility

Sikhs believe that those who gain knowledge of God (who is often called Sat Guru, meaning 'true teacher') see *hukam* (a sense of order, reflecting the will of God) within everything in the world. God is thought of as establishing this order and a Sikh should try to live in harmony with it.

- Can you think of a practical situation in which one of the 'five evil impulses' may be said to make someone blind to truth, and unable to live in natural harmony with the world?

Guidelines for the Sikh way of life are to be found in a short book called the *Rehat Maryada: a guide to the Sikh way of life*, a translation of a book written in Punjabi and published in 1945 by a group of scholars who wanted to summarise the Sikh way of life and the main teachings of the Gurus.

COMMUNITY

After years of travelling and preaching, Guru Nanak settled with his family and followers at Kartarpur. They shared a common life of work and prayer and established a tradition of hospitality. He had a communal kitchen, where the community and its guests ate together, sitting on the floor. Since then this has become an important feature of the Sikh way of life. Every Gurdwara (a Sikh place of worship) has a kitchen (called a *Langar*) and a room where the worshippers can eat together.

In contrast to the caste differences which may separate Hindus, the Sikh community insists on the unity of its members. This is expressed by sitting together in rows to share food (called '*Pangat*'). **A sense of community ('*Sangat*' or 'association') is an important guideline for Sikhs.**

- In what practical ways, and on what occasions, might you use food as a way of expressing friendship?

EQUALITY

All Sikhs are considered equal. There is no separate priesthood, but any Sikh who is suitably educated, may lead the worship in a Gurdwara. All sit together on the floor (usually with men on one side and women on the other) with no-one on special chairs or anything else that might suggest social status. Those of other faiths are also welcome to enter a

Gurdwara and attend a service. They are offered Parshad (a sweet food eaten at the end of worship), and are invited to share the communal meal in the *Langar*.

Although their religion offers a distinctive way of life, Sikhs try never to give offence to those of other faiths. In the Guru Granth Sahib it says:

All men and women are equal – all are children of God

(GGS 611)

and

Who can be called bad, who can be called good? For we see the same God within all.

(GGS 353)

SERVICE

The Sikh guidelines for life emphasise the value of family life and service to others (called 'Seva'). Guru Nanak rejected the idea of the hermit existence, cut off from others, as a way of being religious.

A Sikh has three duties:

1 to bring God to mind (Nam Kapna);
2 to work honestly (Kirat karna);
3 to practise charity (Vand Chhakna).

Service offered to humanity can take three forms:

1 physical (*Tan*) – Sikhs should not rely on charity, but should do useful work.
2 mental (*Man*) – Sikhs should study the Granth, and share their knowledge of it with others, pray, and offer moral support and guidance.
3 material (*Dan*) – Sikhs should give a tenth of their income to religious and charitable work. This is collected and distributed by the Gurdwara.

- Is it easier to be religious when you are quietly on your own, or when working with other people? How does your answer illustrate what you mean by 'religion'?

KHALSA

The last of the ten gurus (Guru Gobind Singh) founded the Khalsa (meaing 'the pure') as a sign of discipline and commitment for adult Sikhs. At the

Amrit ceremony, when a Sikh becomes a member of the Khalsa, the sugar-water used for the 'baptism' is stirred with a sword and the name Singh, given to all men, means 'lion', which suggests strength and discipline.

Of the 'five K's that distinguish a member of the Khalsa, the shorts (*Kachha*) express disipline and readiness (for they are modest and suitable wear for a person who may be called on to fight) and the sword (*Kirpan*) shows that the Sikh is to be a spiritual warrior against the five evil tendencies.

Sikh men (and some Sikh women) have their long, uncut hair (called *Kesh* – itself a sign of dedication) tied up in a turban, so that they are not hindered by it. **Important guidelines expressed by these things are discipline, strength and a willingness to defend the community, even to the point of martyrdom.**

- Do you think it is right for a religion to expect discipline and self-sacrifice from its members, or should it be left to each person's conscience?

SUMMARY OF SIKH GUIDELINES

- *Love God and serve humanity.*
- *Treat all people with equal respect and be charitable towards them.*
- *Defend and support the Sikh community and way of life.*

Over to you

1 Look up details of: the Amrit ceremony; the Khalsa (including how and why it was founded in 1699); the Five 'K's, which show that a Sikh is a member of the Khalsa. These illustrate the general guidelines for the Sikh way of life.
2 Look up the meaning the Sikh symbol, which can be seen on the flag (the *Nishan Sahib*) which is flown outside every Gurdwara.
3 Try to visit (or read about) a Gurdwara. Notice the style of worship, the respect that is shown to the Sikh holy book (the *Guru Granth Sahib*) and the way in which the community organises its *Langar* – with people sharing in the work of preparing food and clearing up after the meal.

Marriage and the family

Guru Nanak taught that God was to be found at home, within oneself and in one's relationships with others. He therefore rejected the Hindu tradition of forsaking worldly comforts and activities (asceticism) in order to pursue religion. He married (as did all the gurus, except Guru Har Krishen, who died as a child) and had a family. When he established his community at Kartapur, his followers lived and worked together in families. **Sikhs therefore see no spiritual benefit in remaining single and it is expected that all will marry.**

MARRIAGE

In the Rehat Maryada it says that caste or birth should be of no account in choosing a marriage partner. The only rules are that a Sikh's daughter should marry a Sikh and that the couple should have reached mental and physical maturity. In the Punjab, a girl must be at least 18 and a boy 20, before they can marry.

It is traditional for the choice of partner to be made by the whole family. This is because, in an extended family, a new daughter-in-law will have to get on with the other women in the family, with whom she will share a kitchen. A bride's parents are also concerned that she should be received into a Sikh family where she would be happy and well treated. This means, in practice, that family wealth, education and caste background can still be important for deciding who is suitable as a marriage partner. The couple themselves have to agree to the marriage, but the parents assist them in their choice.

Before marriage, a couple will not usually spend time alone together, but will meet only when other members of their families are present. There is no need for a formal engagement, but the girl's parents may call on the prospective bridegroom and present him with gifts, usually a *kirpan* (a small sword), and sometimes a *kara* (bangle) and sweets. The prospective bride may also receive presents at this time from the boy's parents. Sometimes the engagement is more formal: it may take place in a Gurdwara and the girl may receive an engagement ring.

The girl's family arrange and pay for the wedding. Sikhs do not allow a cash dowry to be paid by either family.

In the wedding ceremony (called the *Anand Karaj* or 'ceremony of bliss'), the couple are reminded of their duties of love and loyalty to one another and that they should share both their sorrows and their joys. They are also advised to love and respect each other's relatives.

The relationship between husband and wife is described as being like that between God and a believer. **The ideal of Sikh marriage, as expressed by Guru Amar Das, is that the couple will become one spirit within two bodies,** so that they can be happy together, even in times of hardship.

The husband, as head of the household, is required to love and respect his wife, accepting her as an equal partner in their marriage. The wife is required to love and support her husband and to be loyal to him.

Although unusual, a Sikh may marry a non-Sikh, provided that the partner shows an interest in following the Sikh way of life.

Bowing before the Guru Granth Sahib (the Sikh holy book), the bride's father or guardian places the groom's scarf in her hand and the couple are symbolically tied together. Then, while each of the four verses of the Lavan (marriage prayers in the Guru Granth Sahib) are read out and sung, the couple walk round the holy book, still tied together by the scarf.

- One spirit in two bodies – do you think this is a realistic goal for married life? Is it what you would want from a marriage?

Sikh families are patriarchal, which means that the eldest man is regarded as head of the household (and on the death of his father, the eldest son therefore accepts this position). Women are seen as having a supportive role, although, in the Sikh religion, they are equal with men, both personally and spiritually. The Guru Granth Sahib has many positive things to say about women in relation to childbearing and forming a home.

- Can men and women be equal, if a man is always head of the household?
- What are the advantages or disadvantages of the Sikh patriarchal system?

PARENTHOOD

In traditional Sikh culture, birth control is rare. A young couple will be anxious to have a family and particularly to have a son because they hope he will grow up to earn money and support them in their old age, whereas a daughter will leave home when she marries.

In an extended family, children have more adults (uncles, aunts and grandparents) to look after them than in a nuclear family, where parents and children live on their own. Orphans may often have a wider family to care for them.

There is a tradition that family property should be held in common and should pass from one generation to the next without being sold or broken up. Even in Sikh communities in the West, where the whole family may not live together, different parts of a family may combine to buy a business or a piece of property, to be used for their mutual benefit.

ADULTERY AND DIVORCE

Adultery is forbidden in the Sikh religion. The Rehat Maryada says that:

> A Sikh should respect another man's wife as he would his own mother; and another man's daughter as his own daughter.

A promise not to commit adultery is included in the Amrit ceremony, when a Sikh becomes a member of the Khalsa.

Divorce is rare among Sikhs, as in other cultures where marriage is arranged or assisted by the families and where the couple live within an extended family. After divorce, the wife generally returns to her parents' home. Sikhs normally have only one marriage partner, but widows and widowers are allowed to remarry.

- Why do you think divorce is less common among Sikhs than in Western society as a whole?

CARE OF THE ELDERLY

In Guru Nanak's day, Hindu widows were often shunned, being considered a sign of bad luck. Others were encouraged to commit *sati* (the tradition that a wife should commit suicide by throwing herself upon her husband's funeral pyre).

By contrast, Nanak banned *sati* and said that widows should be treated with respect. In the extended family, elderly people are helped by their children and grandchildren, with whom they live and a widow is generally cared for by her eldest son.

ABORTION

Infanticide (the killing of a new-born child) is condemned in the Rehat Maryada. In the time of the Gurus, when male babies brought hope of future prosperity but females offered only a financial burden, there was a temptation to kill baby girls. The Sikh prohibition of this reflected the equality of men and women in the Sikh tradition and the rule that a Sikh should care for all forms of life. It follows from this that the Sikh religion does not approve of abortion.

Over to you

1 Imagine a dialogue between a son who wants to leave the family home, to set up his own family with his wife and child, and his parents, who want him to stay. What arguments might each use in favour of the extended or the nuclear family?
2 List those features of life for young women in the West today which Sikh girls would have to reject if they were to remain faithful to the Sikh religion and culture. (It may be useful to think about the sort of life that is shown in articles and advertisements in women's magazines.)

Peace and conflict

INDIVIDUAL VIOLENCE

Every member of the Khalsa is required to carry a *kirpan* (sword). Some have only a symbolic kirpan, perhaps in the form of a brooch. Others carry a kirpan which could be used as a weapon, but this does not mean that Sikhs approve of violence. **Guru Gobind Singh told his followers never to be the first to draw a sword, so a Sikh may use a kirpan (or any other weapon) only as a means of self-defence.** Sikhs argue that it is right to use violence only in defence of the Sikh community, or in order to help those who are suffering injustice. Anger is one of the evil impulses to be avoided and a Sikh should therefore never use a weapon in anger, but only in order to see that justice is done and then only when all peaceful means of doing so have failed.

In Britain, the law permits Sikhs to wear a turban rather than a crash helmet when riding a motorcycle; this was agreed after protests from the Sikh community. No legislation yet makes special allowance for Khalsa Sikhs who carry a kirpan and young Sikhs are sometimes accused of carrying an offensive weapon, in spite of the fact that it is required by their religion and represents a moral and spiritual fight.

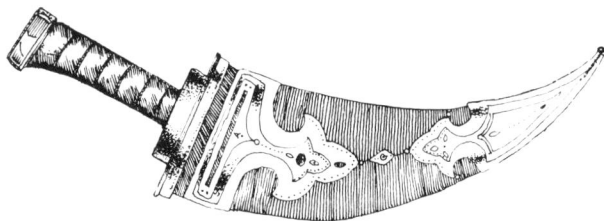

- Is a kirpan an offensive weapon? What defence might a member of the Sikh religion offer against this charge?

ARDAS

The prayer Ardas is an important part of Sikh worship. In it they remember those who have been martyred for their religion.

In its early days, the Sikh community was persecuted from time to time by the Muslim rulers. (The Punjab, where Sikhism developed, was part of the Mughal Empire.) Because of this, Sikhs developed a tradition of military discipline and a concern for the unity and protection of the Sikh community (the Panth).

In the prayer Ardas, Sikhs also pray that they may be united with one another in love, that they may be saved from the five evil impulses and that they may helped in keeping themselves pure. They pray for the welfare of everyone, not just for those of their own community.

POLITICAL ACTION

The Sikh community has suffered as a result of the political as well as the religious changes in the Punjab. The Gurus came under persecution from the Muslim rulers of the Mughal Empire, who, from time to time, tried to force the Sikhs to convert to Islam. There was an independent Sikh state in the Punjab from 1799 to 1839, ruled by Maharajah Ranjit Singh, after which time the area was ruled by the British. At the time of the partition of India in 1947, much of the Punjab, with its population of Sikhs, was made part of Pakistan, the area reserved for Muslims. In the fighting between the two religious and cultural communities that followed, about half a million Sikhs were killed.

Today, the Indian state of Punjab has a majority of Sikhs in its population. The Akali Dal party presses for more independence from India, but the more extreme, militant Sikhs want to set up their own state (which they call Khalistan, 'Land of the Pure') by force. Both in 1984 and 1988, the Golden Temple in Amritsar, the holiest place for Sikhs, was the scene of violence between these Sikh extremists and the Indian army.

- What religious dilemmas might face a person who wants to fight to establish Khalistan?

NON-VIOLENCE

In 1922, the British rulers in India passed a law making it illegal for Sikhs to wear their kirpans. This was resisted by non-violent means, with Sikhs allowing themselves to be beaten for defying the law. Eventually, after four months, the ban on kirpans was lifted.

Many Sikhs were involved in the struggle against British rule in India and supported Mahatma Gandhi. More recently, when Mrs Indira Gandhi, then Prime Minister of India, suspended the democratic government and imposed emergency regulations between 1976 and 1978, Sikhs protested peacefully against this until democracy was restored.

Sikhs are therefore divided about the value of violent and non-violent means of righting what they see as injustice.

- In the face of an oppressive political situation, which would you use non-violent means, or violent self-defence?

Sikhs in London, protesting at the storming of the Golden Temple at Amritsar in 1984.

MINORITY RIGHTS

Nanak rejected the authority of the Hindu Vedas and of the Brahmin priests who interpreted them, believing that God could be known by anyone. He rejected caste differences; the Sikh community eats together (Pangat) as a sign of equality.

The popularity of the Khalsa, when it was first formed, was partly the result of the new sense of equality and self respect that it offered to those of the lower castes.

Women take a full and equal part in Sikh life and worship. They are not veiled or kept in Purdah (a Muslim custom), although modesty in dress is expected.

All people, whether Sikh or non-Sikh are therefore given the same rights and offered the same charity and hospitality by the Sikh community.

In the Punjab, there is often tension between the Sikh and Hindu populations and also between those who support the militants in their struggle for independence and those who take a more moderate line. Such tension sometimes leads to violence. This is caused by the social and political situation there and does not reflect the teachings of the Sikh religion.

WARFARE

According to Sikh belief, warfare is justified in defence of the Sikh people, but only when all other means of securing peace fail.

Since the time of Guru Hargobind, the Sikh people have been armed and prepared for self-defence. This was emphasised by Guru Gobind Singh when he formed the Khalsa, with its tradition of military discipline and the willingness to give one's life in defence of the Sikh religion and people.

Guru Nanak himself may have been pacifist, claiming that, if someone ill-treated you, you should bear it three times and on the fourth time God himself would fight for you. Those who continued this tradition, rejecting the requirements of the Khalsa, were called Nanak-panthis.

The majority of Sikhs, following Guru Nanak's advice that they should live in an honourable way, consider that they can maintain their self-respect only by being prepared to defend themselves by force if necessary.

- Do you think a Sikh would want to impose limitations on the way a war should be fought? What might not be acceptable?

Over to you

1 Look up the history of the Sikh people in a textbook and note down the periods of persecution. How might these experiences of suffering influence the modern debate about the formation of an independent Sikh state (Khalistan).
2 Look up details of the massacre at Amritsar in 1919. In what way might this have contributed to the subsequent history of Sikhism in the Punjab?

Humankind and nature

Sikhs are required to be kind to people, animals and birds. This comes from the conviction that God created everything and that through nature he provides for people's needs.

> From the True one was born the air,
> From air came out water,
> Water brought forth life
> And God prevailed in all His creation.
>
> The Lord who created the world is the Lord of all,
> Whose form is subtle, whose name is the Bright One, and whose image is in all minds.
> He continues to give us our daily bread which never fails.
> (Guru Granth Sahib)

Sikhs should therefore show respect towards nature and gratefulness for what it provides. The Punjab is the richest farming area in India and is more than self-sufficient in food.

Sikhs also believe that all natural forms come from God and will return to him, just as sparks rise from a fire and then fall back to earth, or as waves merge in the single ocean of water.

WORK AND LEISURE

The Rehat Maryada says that no form of work should be thought of as below one's dignity. Therefore a Sikh should be prepared to do anything to serve the community or humanity at large. A practical expression of this is a willingness to help clean the gurdwara and serve food in the langar.

In the guidelines for selecting a husband, honest work is seen as more important than wealth. In one of his hymns, Guru Nanak said:

> Work hard and share your earnings.
> Nanak thou shalt find the way.
>
> Live by the sweat of your brow,
> Earn and deserve all comforts.

In their leisure time, young Sikhs in Britain may join a Sikh youth club, play table tennis, snooker and other activities. They may also be encouraged to learn to play musical instruments, so that they can join the *ragis* (musicians) who lead worship in the gurdwara.

Following the military discipline of the Khalsa, sports which improve physical fitness (e.g. hockey; wrestling; athletics) are particularly encouraged, as is horsemanship.

Two restrictions on leisure:
• Sikhs are not allowed to gamble.
• Sikh parents will probably discourage their children from socialising with those of the opposite sex.

• Why do you think the Sikh religion forbids gambling? (Hint – look up the 'Five evil impulses')

FOOD, DRINK AND DRUGS

The Rehat Maryada prohibits alcohol, tobacco, drugs or other intoxicants and all Sikhs have to promise to obey this rule when they become members of the Khalsa. In the Guru Granth Sahib it says:

> One fills the cups and the other enjoys drinking,
> Little caring that it defiles the intellect and interferes with the constitution.
> Since he cannot differentiate between strangers and kinsmen
> He is hatefully discarded.

Two arguments are expressed here:
- Excessive alcohol harms body and mind.
- When drunk, a person is careless of others.

There are no strict food laws in Sikhism, but many Sikhs are vegetarian and therefore it is usual for gurdwaras to serve vegetarian food, so as not to offend them. Animals should be killed at a single stroke (in other words, as quickly and painlessly as possible) and Sikhs are forbidden to eat meat that has been killed by ritual slaughter (*halal*), according to either the Muslim or the Jewish rites.

Two reasons are given for this:
- That the methods used are cruel (Muslims and Jews deny this).
- It shows that the Sikh has not converted to the other religions, nor accepted the authority of their food laws.

Out of consideration for their Hindu neighbours, by whom the cow is especially respected, most non-vegetarian Sikhs will not eat beef.

A langar in India.

HELPING THE POOR

Guru Amar Das (the third guru) ordered that a free kitchen (*langar*) should be attached to every gurdwara. This does not just serve food after worship, or on special occasions, but may offer a source of food and shelter to those who need it. Particularly in the Punjab, gurdwaras also provide guest rooms for travellers, and run hospitals and other charitable institutions. This is financed by the ten per cent of personal wealth that every Sikh is required to contribute to charity.

Indian Samaritan carries salvation for the destitute on his back

FIFTY-FOUR years ago, a young child lay abandoned on a roadside in Lahore. He was deaf, mute and deformed – a cripple, which in those parts is called a *pingal*. Like countless others in the cruel margins of Indian life, he had been left to die.

Instead, he was taken up, quite literally, by a young man named Puram Singh, who placed the infant on his back and for the next 14 years carried him about north-west India. When the country was divided in 1947, they became part of the flood of refugees which washed into the frontier city of Amritsar.

Since then, Bhagat (devotee of God) Puram Singh has become a local legend.

Taking his inspiration from General William Booth, founder of the Salvation Army, he has built an extraordinary series of refuges for the wretched of the earth.

Now 84, he still tramps the streets of the troubled city, begging money to feed his growing family of destitutes. There are about 300 of them now, cared for in four centres called Pingalwara (home for the cripple).

In the main one, still lives the original Pingal: an old man now, hunched and twisted in his chair, and incapable of speech. 'Look here, this is my friend who rode on my back for all those years,' says Bhagat Puram Singh? 'he is how it all started'.

Derek Brown,
The *Guardian* 22-7-88

- Sikhs take inspiration from the writings of those of other religions, and the Guru Granth Sahib contains hymns written by Hindus and Muslims as well as Sikhs. How is this illustrated in the ideas of Bhagat Puram Singh.

Over to you

After reading through the passage about Bhagat Puram Singh, go through the general guidelines for the Sikh way of life, and list those which can be illustrated from the work of the Bhagat.

Suggested reading

There are many general books on personal and social issues suitable for GCSE students. Those listed here have been selected because they relate specifically to the contribution of one or more of the world religions to those issues.

Most books on individual world religions also contain some relevant information, and students may need to refer to these for the religious ideas and attitudes that shape their moral guidelines.

The books listed here represent no more than a personal selection. Those suitable mainly for background information for teachers are marked *.

Books giving information on social issues in more than one of the world religions:

Religions of Man   J. R. S. Whiting (Stanley Thomas 1983)
The Assisi Documents   (World Wildlife Fund 1986)
Marriage and the Family   J. Prickett (Lutterworth 1985)
Frontiers   R. Gower (Lion 1983)
Religious Beliefs and Moral Codes   J. R. Bailey (Schofield and Sims 1988)
GCSE Religious Studies   J. Jenkins (Heinemann)
Facing the Issues   B. Wintersgill (Macmillan 1987)
Man's Religious Quest   ed Whitfield Foy (The Open University 1978)*

Books giving the contribution of a particular religion to the issues:

Judaism
Jewish Belief and Practice   Jan Thompson (Edward Arnold 1983)
Abortion – a Jewish Response   (Reformed Synagogues of Great Britain 1984)
Jewish Values   ed G. Wigoder, Israel Pocket Library (Keter Publishing House, Jerusalem 1976)
Jews: Their Religious Beliefs and Practices   A. Untermann (Routledge and Kegan Paul 1981)*
Halakah in a Theologian Dimension   D. Novak (Brown University Press 1985)*

Christianity
Christian Belief and Practice   Jan Thompson (Edward Arnold 1982)
Christianity: an approach for GCSE   K. O'Donnell (Edward Arnold 1988)
Framework   M. A. Chignell (Edward Arnold)
Perspectives   M. A. Chignell (Edward Arnold)
Humanae Vitae   (Papal Encyclical 1968)
Christian Ethics   C. Erricker (Chichester Project 1984)
Who Cares?   F. G. Herod (Methuen 1972)

For the Roman Catholic teaching on personal and social issues, there is the series of pamphlets issued by The Catholic Truth Society, 38/40 Eccleston Square, London SW1V 1PD.

Islam
Islamic Belief and Practice   Jan Thompson (Edward Arnold 1981)
Islam: an approach for GCSE   Jan Thompson (Hodder and Stoughton 1990)
Selection from Hadith   A. H. Siddique (Islamic Book Publishers, Kuwait 1987)
Islam – Faith and Practice   M. Ahsan (Islamic Foundation, 223 London Road, Leicester LE2 1ZE 1977)
The Natural Form of Man   A. Bewley (Ta-Ha Publications 1986)
The Muslim Women's Dress   J. R. Badawi (Ta-Ha Publications)
Islam and Social Responsibility   T. B. Irving (Islamic Foundation 1974)
Polygamy in Islamic Law   J. A. Badawi (American Trust Publications 1972)
Approaches to Islam   R. Tames (John Murray 1982)
Islam – its meaning and message   ed K. Ahmed (Islamic Foundation 1975)
Qur'an: basic teachings   ed Irving/Ahmed/Ashan (Islamic Foundation 1979)
Women in Islam   N. Minai (John Murray 1981)
The Essential Teachings of Islam   ed K. Brown and M. Palmer (Rider 1987)
The Muslim Guide   M. Y. McDermott and M. M. Ashan (The Islamic Foundation revised ed 1986)

Caring for Muslims and their Families: Religious Aspects of Care A. Henley (DHSS and King's Fund: available from the National Extension College, 18 Brooklands Avenue, Cambridge CB2 2HN)

Hinduism
Hindu Belief and Practice Damodar Sharma (Edward Arnold)
Approaches to Hinduism R. Jackson and D. Killingley (John Murray 1988)
Hinduism R. C. Zaehner (O.U.P. 1966)*
An Introduction to Krishna Consciousness ed Raghubir dasa and Jnana dasa (The Bhaktivedanta Book Trust)
Hinduism in Great Britain ed R. Burghart (Tavistock Publications 1987)*
Ahimsa Unto Tähtinen (Rider 1976)*
Hinduism in England ed D. G. Brown (Bradford College 1981)*
Caring for Hindus and their Families: Religious Aspects of Care A. Henley (National Extension College)

Buddhism
Buddhist Teachings and Practice M. R. Thompson (Edward Arnold)
A Buddhist's Manual H. Saddhatissa (British Mahabodhi Society 1976)

The Dhammapada trans Juan Mascaro (Penguin 1973)
Buddhism for Today Dharmachari Subhuti (Windhouse Publications; 1988, 2nd ed)*
Buddhism, World Peace and Nuclear War Sangharakshita (Windhorse Publications 1984)
Buddhism and the Cosmos Daisaku Ikeda (Macdonald 1985)*
The Presence and Practice of Buddhism ed P. Connolly and C. Ericker (West Sussex Institute of Higher Education 1985)*

Sikhism
Sikh Belief and Practice M. R. Thompson (Edward Arnold)
Caring for Sikhs and their Families: Religious Aspects of Care A. Henley (National Extension College)
A Sikh Family in Britain W. Owen Cole (RMEP (2nd ed) 1985)
The Sikhs and Their Way of Life Gurinder Singh Sacha (Sikh Missionary Society 1988)
An Introduction to Sikhism G. S. Sidhu (The Sikh Missionary Society 1973)*
Rehat Maryada: a guide to the Sikh way of life trans Kanwaljit Kaur and Indarjit Singh (The Sikh Cultural Society 1971)

Word list

The letters following words in the list below refer to one of the five religions covered in this book, i.e. Sk=Sikh, I=Islam, etc.

Anand karaj (Sk) – 'ceremony of bliss', a wedding

annulment (C) – the declaration that a marriage is not valid, allowing the partners to separate and marry again (used in the Roman Catholic Church)

artha (H) – wealth, material happiness

ascetic – one who does without physical pleasure for spiritual benefit

Ashramas (H) – the stages in a person's life; traditionally there are four of them

Bet Din (J) – a court of three Jewish rabbis

chuppah (J) – the canopy under which a wedding ceremony is performed

dana (B) – the offering of gifts (especially to monks)

democracy – a political system within which individuals can participate, either directly, or through elected representatives

Dharma (B) – teaching; religious principles; the order seen in life

dhimmi (I) – a non-Muslim living in a Muslim country

dhukka (B) – suffering; dissatisfaction with life; first of the Four Noble Truths of Buddhism

esho funi (B) – the dependence of each thing upon its environment

ethics – the study of moral ideas

get (J) – a divorce document, drawn up by a Jewish court

Hadith (I) – traditions associated with the Prophet Muhammad

hakam (Sk) – the sense of order in the universe, believed by Sikhs to have been established by God

halakah (J) – the 'path'; a way of life following the traditions given in the Talmud

halal (I) – 'permitted'; used especially of food

haram (I) – 'not permitted'; anything forbidden to a Muslim

harijan (H) – 'child of God'; used of 'untouchables' or 'outcastes'

hijab (I) – a veil, traditionally worn by women in public

hima (I) – a conservation area, for the protection of the environment and wildlife

himsa (H) – harm; damage done to another creature

hudud (I) – the most severe Muslim punishments

iddah (I) – the waiting period before a divorce can take effect

Ijmah (I) – an agreement on a point on Muslim law

jati (H) – a sub-caste, often based on the work a person does

Jihad (I) – Holy War; also used of internal spiritual struggle

kama (H) – physical pleasure

karma (B, H) – 'actions', good or bad, which produce results for an individual, influencing spiritual progress

kedushin (J) – marriage

khalifa (I) – one who exercises authority on behalf of Allah

khalsa (Sk) – 'pure', use of those who have received Amrit baptism

Kingdom of God (C) – the rule of God on Earth

kirpan (Sk) – a sword

kosher (J) – 'clean'; used of food and other things permitted to Jews

kufr (I) – disbelief in, or ingratitude shown towards Allah

langar (Sk) – communal kitchen, attached to a Gurdwara

mahr (I) – a wedding dowry

mamzer (J) – a person whose parents are not married according to Jewish law

maya (B, H) – illusion

messeder kedushin (J) – the person who conducts a wedding

Middle Way (B) – 4th of the Four Noble Truths; described in the Noble Eightfold Path

Mitzvah (J) – a commandment

moksha (H) – release from the cycle of rebirth

mukti (Sk) – release from rebirth into the presence of God

niroda (B) – 3rd of the Four Noble Truths; the cessation of suffering

nirvana (B) – a state of bliss, beyond desire or rebirth

pangat (Sk) – sitting together in a row to eat, a sign of unity among Sikhs

pansil (B) – the five principles of training, accepted by Buddhists

panth (Sk) – the community

pietists (C) – those who, for religious reasons, will not take part in any political activity

polygamy – the marriage of a man to more than one woman at a time

purdah (I) – the separation of women from men in society

Qadi (I) – the 'judge' who officiates at a wedding

Qur'an (I) – the holy book of Islam, revealed to Muhammad

rabbi (J) – a teacher

samsara (B, H) – rebirth

sangat (Sk) – the community of Sikhs

Sangha (B) – the community of monks

sati (H) – a wife's suicide on her husband's funeral pyre

seva (Sk) – service offered to others; physical, mental and material

Shalom (J) – 'peace'

Shari'ah (I) – 'the way'; used of Islamic law

shirk (I) – associating something with God; idolatry

shochet (J) – a person trained to carry out the slaughter of animals according to the Jewish tradition

Sin (C) – the separation of a person from God

Sunnah (I) – the example of the Prophet Muhammad; used as a guideline by Muslims

Talmud (J) – books of commentary on the Jewish law (Torah)

tanha (B) – 'craving'; the cause of suffering; 2nd of the Four Noble Truths

tauhid (I) – the natural unity of all things in Allah

Tenaim (J) – engagement to be married

Torah (J) – the Law; used of the first five books in the Bible; the basis of Jewish guidelines

tughyan (I) – unnatural activity, showing a failure to trust Allah

ummah (I) – the Muslim community

varna (H) – 'colour'; used of the four major Hindu caste groups

zakah (I) – money given to charity, required of all Muslims

Zedakah (J) – 'justice'; used of gifts of charity

Index

Entries in bold refer to issues on which more than one religion offer guidelines.
Numbers in italics refer to illustrations.